# DID YOU KNOW THAT YOU ARE RUNNING YOUR OWN LIFE?

If you are an aware person, you are constantly searching for answers to the most fundamental challenges of living. But have you considered that as your awareness increases, your control over your entire being increases? And once you become aware that you are choosing everything, you can take over your own life and live it the way your inner self *knows* how to live it?

*PROFOUND SIMPLICITY*
will help to show you the way.

## ABOUT THE AUTHOR

WILL SCHUTZ, Ph.D., has taught and conducted research at Harvard University, the University of Chicago, the University of California at Berkeley, and at the Albert Einstein Medical School. He is the author of *Firo* (*The Interpersonal Underworld*), the bestselling *Joy, Here Comes Everybody, Body Fantasy, Elements of Encounter,* and *Leaders of Schools.* Now engaged in consulting and writing in northern California, he tries to blend the experiential and the scientific, the East and the West, both in his work and in his life. He is currently the Director of the Center for Holistic Studies at Antioch University in San Francisco.

# PROFOUND
# SIMPLICITY
## Will Schutz

PROFOUND SIMPLICITY
*A Bantam Book  /  June 1979*

ISBN 0–553–11748–3

*Published simultaneously in the United States and Canada*

*Bantam Books are published by Bantam Books, Inc. Its trade-mark, consisting of the words "Bantam Books" and the por-trayal of a bantam, is Registered in U.S. Patent and Trademark Office and in other countries. Marca Registrada. Bantam Books, Inc., 666 Fifth Avenue, New York, New York 10019.*

PRINTED IN THE UNITED STATES OF AMERICA

# CONTENTS

Prologue 1
Introduction 3

## 1: PRINCIPLES 15
Holism 17
Limitlessness 25
Choice 29
Simplicity 60
Truth 79
Completion 98
Basic Dimensions 111

## 2: APPLICATIONS 139
Principles of Applications 144
Law 149
Medicine 162
Politics 170
Sports 184
Education 192
Family 195
Living 202
Endarkenment 204
Epilogue 206
Notes 207
Index 215

PROLOGUE

# PROLOGUE

"It's incredible. I've never known anyone like you who talks."

"We all can talk for a short time if we want to."

"Will you answer my questions?"

"With pleasure."

"I've been alive a long time and I don't know why. What am I here for?"

"All things, whether they be computers, cities, or flowers, are here to unfold, to become what they are capable of being."

"Ideally, perhaps, but there are so many people that keep me from being what I could be."

"You are the only one keeping you. The choices you make determine the life you lead."

"Do you mean that I choose everything that I do?"

"Exactly. You are running your own life."

"I don't remember deciding to do many of the things I have done. Certainly I wouldn't have done them if I really had a choice."

"You had the choice. You just didn't let yourself know that you were choosing. It seemed to be too much of a burden."

"What you are saying sounds scary. Surely there are limits to my power to decide. I mean, after all, I'm not . . ."

"There are limits only if you believe there are limits. In fact, there are none. You can be anything you wish. And you have no obligation to be anything at all. It's all up to you . . . Please look me in the eye. I feel better when you do."

1

"Sorry . . . You sound a little weary . . . Even if you are right, so what? How could I become all of the things I am?"

"The key is truth."

"Truth? What does truth have to do with it?"

"To function best, you must know yourself. You must be willing to experience what you really are."

"OK. I understand that. What about other people? Can they help?"

"Other people are in the same position that you are . . . Rock me a little, will you? . . . They can help because they are mirrors. There is one requirement, however."

"What is that?"

"You must be honest. If you are to learn from them, and they from you, you must tell each other exactly what you are experiencing. Otherwise, you are simply colluding with each other to deceive yourselves and to keep yourselves blind."

"You seem to be talking slower now."

"Yes, I'm getting weaker. I can talk just a little longer."

"One more thing. Surely everything is much more complicated than you are describing it. There are so many variables in the world."

"No. There are many levels of existence, but they are all just aspects of you. Once you experience yourself fully, that's all there is. Everything is one . . . I'm really fading now. I want to go over there. I'll see you later."

I picked up my newborn son, Ari, and gently placed him on his mother's breast.

# INTRODUCTION

## STYLE

To avoid sexist grammar and to enhance a direct writing style, I shall employ a method I have used in two previous books (*Elements of Encounter*[1] and *Body Fantasy*[2]). For certain descriptions, I shall use "I" for the universal self and "you" for the universal other. This convention avoids the cumbersome he-she-they locutions and the use of "he" or "him" to represent both male and female.

To keep the text simple, I have relegated most references and technical comments to the Notes section in the back of the book. The text should be quite comprehensible without them. References to the Notes are indicated by superscripts.

Many of the methods developed in the human potential movement—methods such as encounter, gestalt, and fantasy—are not well known to the general public. Whenever an understanding of one of these techniques is important for following the ideas, I have provided a brief description in the text or in the appropriate Note. For readers who wish to explore these methods in more detail, Note 7 presents an extensive list of references.

## THE NEW ERA

Humanity is cresting toward a major revolution. The social revolutions of the sixties gave way to the aware-

3

ness explosion of the seventies. From these thrusts is
emerging still another awareness, perhaps the most
significant of all: Each of us is running her or his
own life.

The first era of humankind was based on ignorance
and superstition. We did not know the laws of the
universe, of physics, of psychology, of sociology, of
physiology. We created beliefs and superstitions and we
lived by them.

The scientific revolution substituted knowledge for
ignorance and changed the world. We learned how
nature works and we learned to overcome or to harmonize with it.

Now, a startling realization is dawning—the realization that the laws of nature only function if we want
them to.

All around us people are defying natural laws. Biofeedback subjects alter their blood pressure,[3] cancer
patients stop the growth of their disease,[4] psychics bend
keys and move objects with their minds,[5] and people
respond to jealousy situations without becoming jealous.
We are not required to follow any laws. We are running
this show.

As my awareness increases, my control over my own
being increases. When I am ignorant, I do not let
myself know how to harmonize with the laws of nature.
When I acquire knowledge, I may harmonize with
nature, but I do not necessarily allow myself to know
how to change the things I would like to change. When
I become aware that I am choosing everything, I may
take over my life and live it any way I choose.

I uncover my own power as I become aware and
as I start to tell the truth. The truth makes me free.
The truth leads me to understand how to run my own
life.

The awareness revolution began in several places,
most prominently in a seemingly provincial, primarily
West Coast phenomenon known as the human potential
movement. In the late 1960s, first California, then
America, then the world, was introduced to a series

of theories and techniques aimed at realizing the human potential. In 1976, Adam Smith[6] put the imprimatur of the establishment on these methods by reporting his experiences with some of these techniques. Large segments of the public have responded eagerly to each human potential technique, typically creating a best-selling book and a large following for each method. Encounter, gestalt therapy, rolfing, transactional analysis, bioenergetics, transcendental meditation, psychosynthesis, Arica, relaxation, breathing, T'ai Chi, Aikido, the Alexander technique, Feldenkrais, Trager, jogging, fasting, yoga, Fisher-Hoffman, scintology, primal therapy, Baba Ram Dass, est, and a small covey of gurus and swamis have all taken their places on the American stage in the last decade.[7]

Reaction to this plethora of methods for improving the "quality of life" has been varied. Some observers find in the movement the greatest hope for the elevation and evolution of humankind. Others liken the methods to fads, rising and falling in popularity, then disappearing.

In fact, none of the methods has disappeared; only national media coverage eventually disappears. By definition, each can be news—that is, new—for a limited time only. After public attention diminishes, each method spreads to the hinterlands, both within and without America. Human potential techniques are being applied in prisons, schools, churches, hospitals, businesses, psychotherapy, theater, sports, politics, marriage counseling, married life, childrearing, and even string quartets!

Each method that has achieved popularity has benefited many people. Each technique is a different way of presenting some very profound and very simple ideas—ideas that have been distilled over the centuries and across many lands. Each method appeals to different types of people or to each person at a particular stage of life.

For those who want to be told answers, gurus are ideal for creating conditions which people may use to attain their next level of human evolution. For people who want strong confrontation to stir them from their rudderless journeys, gestalt, encounter, or est fits best. Other people feel dead in their bodies, and they use varied approaches to awaken themselves to feel what is below their necks and to turn on their lives. For such people, rolfing, bioenergetics, Alexander, Trager, or Feldenkrais may be the appropriate method.

The new revolution springs from the old truths. Most answers have been around for centuries: "The truth shall make you free;" "Know thyself;" "Self-responsibility;" "The body is the temple of the soul."

We know all and we know nothing because we do not really believe these truths. What is new is that we are now beginning to believe them and to discover and create the technology that provides the means for us to put them to use in our lives.

The principles underlying the human potential techniques become the lights that penetrate the human dilemma. Their implications are awesome. Applications of these principles to modern society would reweave the cultural fabric. Medicine would be refined and expanded; government would be totally chaotic until it settled down into great clarity and directness; law, welfare programs, economics, athletic events, religion, taxation, family life, education, industry, and human relations, even our mortality, would be deeply affected.

This book is an effort to divine the profound simplicities lurking beneath the many approaches to the realization of a human being's full potential, to integrate these principles with the scientific method where appropriate, and to describe a few examples of the application of these principles to modern existence.

To set the background for this exploration I will tell you of my own experience with human potential techniques and with academic science:

Student at UCLA under Hans Reichenbach and Abraham Kaplan on scientific method.

Fifteen years of academic, scientific research

as a faculty member at Harvard, Chicago, Berkeley, Tufts, Einstein Medical School, and currently at Antioch University in San Francisco. Awarded eight research contracts from government and private agencies (Office of Education, Office of Naval Research, Rosenberg Foundation).

Twenty years of conducting encounter groups in this country and in Australia, Canada, England, France, Germany, Holland, Israel, Mexico, New Zealand, Nigeria, Puerto Rico, and Sweden.

Twenty years of consulting in business, government, education, and community organizations.

Six hundred hours in Psychoanalysis.

Ten sessions in didactic Psychosynthesis.

One year in Bioenergetic therapy.

Forty-three Rolfings.

est basic training.

Forty-day Arica training.

Readings from and training with Jack Schwarz, a psychic.

Training in Acupuncture theory.

Training in the Feldenkrais theory and exercises.

Qualified as a Rolf practitioner.

Qualified as a Zone Therapy practitioner.

Qualified member of the American Group Psychotherapy Association.

Qualified member (since 1950) of the American Psychological Association.

I have had my Tarot read, my I Ching thrown, my horoscope analyzed, my biorhythms charted, and my irises interpreted (Iridology). I have had darshan with Bhagwan Rajneesh in Poona, India. I have had mantras intoned on my chakras. Fritz Perls has gestalted me, Ida Rolf has rolfed me, and Alexander Lowen has done bioenergetics on me. I have been structurally patterned by Judith Aston, been shown Aikido and been Alexandered. Alan Watts, Abraham Maslow, Carl Rogers, and Rollo May have lectured to me. I have meditated at a Zen Center (Tassajara), done yoga regularly for six months, learned T'ai Chi (short form), jogged about three miles a day for six year, seen auras, astrally projected, taken most of the known psychedelic drugs, and fasted for 34 days on distilled water. And I knew Timothy Leary when he just smoked cigarettes and Ram Dass (Richard Alpert) when he shaved.

## THE JOYFUL LIFE

John Dewey once said that every theory needs one unprovable assumption. After that, all statements are ultimately testable.

The unprovable assumption in the present philosophy is this: My ultimate aim as a human being is a joyful life. Joy is the feeling that results from using myself, my thinking and feeling capacities, my senses, my body and my spirit, in all the ways of which I am capable. I am less happy when I am not using myself and when I am blocking myself.[8]

When pollsters ask the public for its goal for humankind, the most popular answer is peace. For me, peace is too puny a goal when compared to our capacities. As a social goal, peace is simply absence of war; as a personal goal, absence of turmoil. The experience of joy transcends absence of the negative.

The goal of joy reflects the human potential movement as contrasted with more traditional psychotherapy. Many years ago, I worked in a mental hospital as a psychologist alongside several psychiatrists. We had a running argument. I was appalled when I observed what the psychiatrists referred to as a normal family. Communication among family members was almost nonexistent, they were not nourishing to each other, all seemed to be operating at a minor fraction of their capacities, and they were cheerless. In what sense was this a normal family?

The psychiatrists saw them as normal because in the family there was no alcoholism, no crime, no drug problems, no child abuse, no reading difficulties, and no mental illness. It became clear that we had different criteria. The psychiatric objective is to get a family or a person from minus to zero; mine is to get a family or a person from minus to plus.

The philosophy of the joyful life also differs from those Eastern philosophies and religions based on sacrifice to attain higher consciousness. In those approaches, lower center activities, such as sexuality and competition, are foregone so that energy may be channeled into the higher, spiritual centers. I want all centers flowing fully so that sexuality and spirituality, competition and affection, intellect and feeling, all function optimally. I see no need and have no wish for the suppression of any capacity for the sake of another.

The full experience of joy requires total awareness of myself and of my capacities. I am aware of each part of myself and I am able to control each part independent of all other parts. I deal with each new situation by organizing my entire being to meet it in the way I wish to meet it. At each moment, I am able to put my body in any state I wish. I can will mystical experiences, psychedelic states, body awareness, or anything I choose. I can do it without the aid of mechanical aids or drugs. I can do it by just deciding to do it. When I achieve total awareness, down to my smallest unit of existence, I am totally in the now at each point. And since everything is in each thing—the macrocosm in the microcosm—I am everywhere, I am omniscient, I am God.[9] This is the full experience of joy.

## BELIEF

I am about to make many statements that may seem bizarre, statements that call into question many of the assumptions both you and I have believed for many years. If believing something means that I spontaneously behave consistently with that belief, then I believe very little of what I am about to say.

A few years ago, my son Caleb, then sixteen years old, told me he wanted to drop out of high school. Having the self-image of a liberal, bordering on wonderful, parent, I took his announcement with ostentatious equanimity. "Of course, it is your decision," I explained. "If that is what you want to do, I certainly support you." Pause. "I'm sure you realize," I howevered, "that you may not be able to get a job as good as the one you would get if you finished school. After all, you only have a year and a half to go. Don't you think—"

"Dad, what are you saying? I heard you lecture the other night, and you talked about the irrelevance of most of education."

"Well, I—"

"And you said people should follow their own energy. I have no energy for school. I hate to go to school. But I stay up until two in the morning working on this job I have. And I go bowling every night."

After I recovered from the momentary shock of "Oy, my son the bowler!" I smiled tightly, told him to be quiet, and excused myself. It took only a moment to realize that Caleb was right. For years, through the spoken and written word, I had been enunciating these principles. When it came to responding on a personal level, however, I reacted as my father would have reacted thirty years before. An image of myself as a thermometer leapt into my head. My belief in the principles I championed extended from the top of my head down to about my throat. If I have to answer an intellectual question about the relevance of education, I am sparklingly consistent with my publicly stated beliefs. If my belief is measured by my spontaneous response when the situation involves my heart or the deep feelings residing in my abdomen, my "gut feelings," apparently I do not believe those principles at all.

This unnerving revelation led me to muse about all the beliefs I had written and spoken about for years. Alas, it was true for all of them. I have espoused complete honesty, yet I recognize situations where my stomach is tight, my throat is dry, and my voice is taut when I am being honest. Those parts of my body do not fully believe the honesty principle.

The books I have written are beginnings of beliefs. They state what my head accepts. The rest of my being accepts what I have written only in a chaotic, jigsaw fashion, parts of me accepting the belief, parts having no knowledge of the belief, and parts quite opposed to the belief. Later, when I was exposed to the Feldenkrais method[7] (see page 189), the partial nature of my belief became clearer.

Feldenkrais exercises require harmonious body movement. One exercise in particular is quite acrobatic. As I gradually mastered coordination of my arms, hands, legs, shoulders, and head, I experienced a wonderfully peaceful, light, balanced, open feeling. "How joyful!" I reflected. "I feel joy when I am doing what I am capable of doing, when I am realizing my potential." That thought had a familiar ring. "By God, that's the way I defined joy nine years ago.[8] So that's what I meant!"

The feeling was very clear. The definition I offered in *Joy* was exactly correct, but at the time of writing it, I had little experience of what I meant. I had not *knowingly* experienced joy. Now, seven years later, I was feeling what I already knew with my head. Subsequently, I have found the same thing to be true of virtually all my writing. A book of mine is a preview of what I am about to experience.

What seems to happen is a three-step process. I first experience something without awareness, e.g., the feeling of joy when I do what I am capable of. Later, when I formulate a concept, or when I hear someone else's concept (see, for example, Rajneesh's concept on page 195), I am guided by my own experience, still not aware of its connection to my earlier experience. This occurred when I defined "joy." The final stage unites the experience with the intellectual formulation, as when I did the Feldenkrais exercise. At this time, my organism becomes integrated and experience and awareness of the experience happen simultaneously.

I *truly* believe an idea when my spontaneous reactions are consistent with that belief. My response to Caleb was not consistent with the belief that a person should follow his or her energy. Had it been, I would have spoken and felt in a manner supportive of his desire. My heart would have felt open, my stomach relaxed, and my words supportive. In fact, only my words were supportive, and then only after Caleb had confronted me about my first response, and only after I had taken time for reflection.

The ideas in this book are offered in this sense of belief. With my head, I believe they are true. I am convinced their truth ultimately will come to be widely recognized. I am absolutely certain of it. Yet there are parts of me that do not for a moment believe it. The longer I live with the ideas, realize their implications, and experience the ideas in action, the more I believe them with more of myself.

I offer you these ideas on two levels: hypothesis and belief. You may believe, as I do, that they are true, and/or you may *assume* them to be true and try them out. Some ideas, like "there are no accidents," offer an advantage when you assume them to be true. If you allow yourself to assume, for example, that there are no accidents, then you have an opportunity to discover whether that statement is true. If you assume that many things are the result of chance occurrences, then you will never know whether you have a hand in creating that which occurs in your life. To assume, therefore, is pragmatic.

What became of Caleb? He dropped out of school, his business venture failed, and he started hanging out at bowling alleys. As a result, he became a premier bowler. Then he tired of the whole thing. On his own initiative, he began studying for the high school equivalency exam, passed it, and went to junior college a year and a half ahead of his high school class. He paid for part of his education from his winnings in bowling tournaments. He transferred to the University of California, Santa Cruz, graduated with honors and was admitted to graduate school at UCLA.

# 1

---

# PRINCIPLES

# HOLISM

God wrote not the laws in pages of books, but
in your heart and in your spirit. They are in
your breath, your blood, your bone, in your
flesh, your bowels, your eyes, your ears and in
every little part of your body.

—Jesus Christ[10]


One principle that is widely known and sparsely
believed, is the principle that each one of us is a
unified, integral organism. I am an organism who
manifests through thinking, feeling, sensing, and moving and who has a spiritual aspect. These are not
unrelated functions. My feelings influence my thinking,
my sensitivity to sensations influences my movement.
Illness, too, is a manifestation of my whole being. I
have integrity both in the sense of being whole and in
the sense of being truthful.

There is a strong cultural current recognizing holism.
Holistic health, law, dentistry, politics, business, sports,
and education are beginning to surface in California
and elsewhere.[11]

The retreat from the dualism of mind and body and
the return to the whole person is leading to profound
changes in our understanding of human behavior.

Illness responds best to a total, or holistic, approach.
When cancer experts deal with cancer as if it were
purely a disease of the body, the results are puny. An
authoritative spokesman, after a recent, careful assess-
ment of cancer research, concludes:

After approximately two decades and several billion dollars expended on research for cures (for cancer), official figures on trends in five-year survival rates do not, by any reasonable standard, provide for optimism.

Also, truth was an issue, as he continued:

Finally, I went to another cancer institution, one of the most eminent, where I spoke with a physician who occupies a top administrative post. "The problem is the closed mind of medicine," he said. "Orthodoxy prevails everywhere, and it's hard to get them to listen to a new idea. . . . I'm convinced that for some cancers the survival rates were better decades ago, but don't tell anyone I said that. The official line is that we're making a lot of progress."[12]

Failure to recognize the essential unity of the body-mind leads to inadequate understanding of human behavior. American medicine often concentrates on the specific, final events preceding death rather than on the situations that led to the final blow. Even if the final cause is removed, the life-style that produced the difficulty will continue to propel the person back to the same point or to produce an alternate symptom.

## EYESIGHT

The importance of the need for a unified approach became clear in workshops in which we explored eye problems as a phenomenon of the whole person. As an aftermath of these workshops, two people later wrote me of their experiences. One man used the technique of the guided imagery[13] to explore his near-sightedness:

I had a kind of minor breakthrough when we came home after last weekend's workshop and

Deborah and I were practicing some of the imagery methods. While still at Big Sur on Sunday, I had tried going (in imagery) into my very myopic eyes. I got an image of a wall with broken glass on top, and a rose garden on the other side, which I wanted to get to, but also a wolf which I feared. I couldn't demolish the wall, and didn't know how to deal with the wolf. The wall then became transparent: a perfect symbol of myopia. You first have a wall to avoid seeing something, then you arrange to see through anyway and still keep the wall.

Anyway, after we got home, I decided to ask myself when was the wall built. In doing so, I suddenly flashed on an incident at the age of twelve when I was humiliatingly teased for "rolling my eyes" at a girl. Immediately, a big chunk of tension peeled off my eyes and the side of my face, and my eyes were able to roll in a certain way for the first time in thirty years. Their relative fixity was a major factor in the myopia, which, according to the researches of Simpkin in England, is clearly caused by atrophy of the converging-diverging capacity of the eye.

The cause of myopia was embedded in the childhood incident. The defective musculature was a consequence. Medical approaches—glasses or surgery or even exercises—can do little to alleviate the situation since they are largely irrelevant in that they do not get at the cause.

A dramatic example of the origins of near-blindness came from a man who had only read of the possibility that his sight was a function of his total life-style:

When I read on p. 185 of *Here Comes Everybody*[14] that you strongly urge that eyeglasses not be worn in your groups, and that occasionally some people experienced sporadic perfect vision, I began trembling with excitement, then fear, and then began to cry. (I have 20/400 vision and have lived with glasses since the first grade.) I have always been told by doctors that "there is nothing we can do, your eyes are healthy but simply out of focus with astigmatism."

What was most significant was that as I let myself go with the feelings as I was crying, I had a very clear vision of me as a small child looking up at my mother. She was furious, her eyes were piercing, and she was raging at me because I had just shit in my pants. Apparently, I must have been difficult to toilet train. I now recall that she was holding out the dirty underwear, and then rubbed it in my face as punishment. The next vision I had was staring at myself in the bathroom mirror, sobbing over what I saw—shit sticking to my lips and teeth. I think I felt betrayed and defiled.

I now suspect that that was the last time I saw anything clearly . . . I can't even see the big E on the eye chart, nor anyone's features more than a foot away. But what is exciting is the realization that I must have seen my mother's features very clearly. Assuming that I was about three or maybe four, and maybe two feet high, her face must have been at least four feet from mine. Also, I couldn't have been closer than three feet from the bathroom mirror. Because of the clarity of the flashback, I must have seen her and my own mirrored face very clearly.

As you said in the book, I am responsible for me. Is it possible that I have actually defocused my eyes and kept them that way all these years? . . .

Not only is it possible, but there are several successful techniques based on this type of explanation: the approach of considering the whole organism.[15]

## PERSONALITY AND TISSUE

Another example of holism is the relation between body tissue and personality. They are not simply two different parts of the person. They are manifestations of the same being.

Levels of personality are equivalent to levels of tissue in the body. Psychological defenses are expressed in the pattern of body tensions. The tissue is like the personality. Layers of tissue parallel layers of personality, with the outer layers the most visible part of the personality and the deeper layers the most hidden parts.

Rose was a woman of great sensitivity and lack of subtlety. She was very aware of smells, sunsets, and touches. When someone was being ironic, she usually did not catch on. She took that person literally and was often hurt. When I rolfed her,[16] she could hardly stand it. I barely touched her and she screamed. She bruised easily and could not stand more than five or ten minutes of rolfing at a time, and then she would cry at length.

Karl was tough. He was a hardheaded, practical man whose approach to life was sardonic, a Don Rickles-like insultingly friendly man. Karl was not sensitive, not easily hurt or penetrated. He could not remember the last time he had cried. When I touched his skin, it was like steel. He was literally thick-skinned.

Paul put up a show of toughness yet was soft underneath. When I pressed on his tissue, he felt very firm until I pressed harder. Then he became soft and penetrable, exactly the way his personality expressed itself.

Psychological defenses appear as body tensions. If you fear exposing your heart to others, that is, if you do not allow yourself to feel tenderness, you often will have muscle tension in the chest area. If you defend yourself through intellectualizing, there is almost inevitably going to be a bar of muscle tension in your neck and shoulders which impedes the flow of energy (blood, nerve) between your head and body, between your thinking and your feeling. As you drop your defenses on a psychological level, your body tensions fade.

## BODY FOLK WISDOM

Folk phrases expressing feelings in body terms are literally true. In an earlier book,[8] I listed about fifty phrases that are commonly used to describe emotions in body terms. Here are some others: "both feet on the ground," "on your toes," "dig in your heels," "stiff-necked," "stand on your own two feet," "get a grip on yourself," "behind your back," "gutsy," "have a heart," "beady-eyed," "don't lose your head."

These phrases are literally true. People who are "on their toes," that is, alert and striving, tend to have their body weight far forward on their feet. People who do not "lose their heads," that is, who strive to stay calm, rational, and in control, tend to have tight neck muscles.

Helen came to me complaining that she could not "stand up" to her husband. Her descriptive phrase gave the clue as to where to look in her body for the physical locus of the problem. When I examined her feet, it was clear that it would be very difficult for her to stand up to anyone. Her feet barely touched the ground. Her arch was extremely high and her feet, where they did touch the ground, were very wobbly. I rolfed her feet and lower legs and she made much better contact with the ground.

She was ecstatic and spent the next two days walking barefoot and experiencing a totally new sensation of stability. Later she reported that she "stood up" to her husband much more effectively now that she "had both feet on the ground," her own phrases.

The widespread, accurate use of these body phrases is an indication of the unaware understanding we have of the relation between the emotional and the body levels. This relation is not mysterious. It is obvious. Most people know the connection. They simply do not realize that they know.

## SINS OF THE FATHERS

When a problem is not dealt with at one level of organization, it must be dealt with at the next lower level. Levels are not independent. They are part of the whole.

Schizophrenigenic is a wonderful word that refers to a situation, usually a familial one, from which a schizophrenic person originates. Frequently, these families are found to have conflicts that they do not deal with directly. Focusing on the schizophrenic child allows the parents to ignore their own difficulties. When the child begins to recover, the family often becomes panicky and acts to put the child back into its old role, lest the parents have to face their own difficulties. The child deals with the problems avoided by the parents.

Sharon was divorced and had one small child. Although she was quite young, Sharon's eyes suddenly started to blur and her visual acuity reduced markedly and stayed that way for a year and a half. In an encounter group, she began to discuss her feelings about being a single parent and her anger toward her former husband. She remained calm as she related this. Someone asked her about her feelings toward her son. As Sharon explored this feeling, she became very agitated. Often, she said, she did not like her son. Frequently, she wished he would go away. She resented his interfering with her relations with men and his burdening of her. Then Sharon felt enormous guilt. Good mothers do not have such feelings.

"I don't want to look at my feelings toward him," she cried. As she came to terms with her feelings and began to accept them as all right, she became aware of her phrase. Perhaps that is what she literally did not want to look at, so she tightened her eye muscles and literally could not see well. Two years after this experience, Sharon reports that she sees well enough so that she is no longer required to wear glasses while driving.

These examples have two things in common. One level of organization, family or parent, has a conflict and the conflict is not being dealt with, most likely is not even in awareness. When this occurs, the next lower level of organization, in this case the child and the eyes, must deal with the conflict. When the conflict is brought into awareness, the next lower level is relieved of the problem. The "sins of the fathers" are no longer visited upon the children.

Holism is an approach. It does not preclude detailed examination of parts. Certainly medical knowledge about each organ and cell in the body is of great value. Holism simply says be sure to acknowledge the integrity of the organism.

# LIMITLESSNESS

If the doors of perception were
cleansed, everything would appear to man as
it is, infinite.
For man has closed himself up,
till he sees all things through
narrow chinks of his cavern.

—William Blake[17]

Achieving the joyful life is accomplished by realizing our potentials. What is the extent of this potential? What are our capacities?

As human beings, we are without limit. We use a pathetically small percentage of the capacity of our nervous systems, probably no more than fifteen percent.[18]

As we learn to use more and more of our capacities, we become capable of more and more "impossible" feats. Biofeedback allows us to control our "involuntary" processes. Psychics are emerging from scientific laboratories having demonstrated "superhuman" powers.[19]

Psychic powers are within the ability of us all. I assume that most tales of yogis and holy men are true. They have found ways to transcend what we now consider to be the laws of nature. All of us can learn to do that too.

I suggest that one reason for the immense popularity of the *Guinness Book of World Records*[20] is that people unconsciously know that it describes our present condition of accomplishment. Each of us is capable of accomplishing everything achieved by all the people in that book, which describes the present actualization of humankind.

The assumption of human limitlessness is often resisted because it is assumed to be accompanied by the demand that I live up to my potential. The feeling of guilt over falling short is, however, quite independent of the assumption itself. I may believe both that I have no limits and that it is perfectly all right for me not to realize all my possibilities. If I wish, I can choose to feel inadequate because I have not realized myself fully. But it is not inherent in the assumption of limitlessness that failure to achieve all that is possible must lead to feelings of guilt and depression. I have no obligation to be everything of which I am capable.

To assume limitlessness has pragmatic advantages. If indeed I am truly limitless, and I assume that I am, then I may discover that limitlessness. On the other hand, every limit that I assume I have prevents me from discovering whether that limit is in fact real. The most fruitful assumption, therefore, is that I am limitless.

The limits I do experience are limits of belief, not limits of the human organism. I am limited because I believe I am limited. A clear instance of this occurred about twenty years ago with the Bannister effect. In the early 1950s, several articles by eminent physiologists appeared, describing why it was physically impossible for a human being to run a mile in less than four minutes. Shortly thereafter, Roger Bannister, a human being, ran a mile in less than four minutes. Today hundreds of men have run a mile in less than four minutes, one in more than ten seconds less.

An updated version of this effect was inspired by Uri Geller. Geller is a "spoon-bender" of considerable renown. After a metal-distorting tour of England, media broadcasters asked for similar experiences from the public. Reports flooded in that cutlery all over the country was being assaulted by large numbers of children. These children, hearing that it was possible for *someone* to bend spoons, assumed limitlessness and discovered that they too were capable of these psychic feats.[21]

Parents are often quite accomplished at urging children to accept limits: You are clumsy, you are stupid, you cannot sing, you are selfish, you are sloppy, you are lazy, you are irresponsible, you are a nuisance. As a child, once I accept this characterization and make it my own, it becomes true. It is true not because it is really so, but because I believe it is true. I then live my life as if I were clumsy, lazy, stupid, or irresponsible. I do not question that I am. Every time I do something inept, it confirms that I am. Every time I do something ept, I do not let myself know it, or I assume it is an exception to my true character. I make no attempt to change my behavior since I have convinced myself that I am "just that way."

Of course, all this is nonsense. I was told when I was young that I was a "housewrecker," someone very untalented, even dangerous, when using my hands. I took a course in woodworking in high school and, as I now see it, dutifully did very badly. Knowing before I started how tangle-fingered I was, I proceeded to make myself anxious when instructions were given, anticipating the moment of humiliation when I would be exposed. I watched the other "superior" students, hoping to be able to copy them well enough to get by. Between anxiety and copying, I devoted almost no energy to learning how to build. The disastrous outcome reinforced what I already knew, namely, that I was manually hopeless.

About twenty years later, after not using my hands for building since that traumatic experience, I decided I wanted to build a table for my house. Furtively I went to the garage alone and built it. It was not good, but it seemed retrievable, so I rebuilt it. To my amazement and delight, it looked remarkably like a table. Then I allowed myself to believe that if I looked at it, I, yes, I, the old housewrecker, might have a good idea about building it better. It was an exhilarating experience. I have now built several things, and they are all rather decent.

# CHOICE

> If you are in poor health, you can remedy it.
> If your personal relationships are unsatisfactory, you can change them for the better. If
> you are in poverty, you can find yourself surrounded by abundance. . . . Each of you, regardless of position, status, circumstances or
> physical condition, is in control of your own
> experience.
>
> —Seth[22]

During the early 1960s, I conducted T-groups for
the National Training Laboratories (NTL) at Bethel,
Maine.[23] Many workshops were run at one time, each
comprising groups of about fifteen people. In order to
discharge what was considered to be our professional
responsibility, the director of NTL would open the
session by announcing, in increasingly euphemistic
terms, something to this effect:

"There may be times when you will find the group
experience somewhat stressful and you may feel the
desire to talk to someone about what is happening to
you. For this purpose, there will be a counselor available in Room 104 between four and six o'clock. Be
sure to use him if you feel the need."

On the average, about two-thirds of the participants
in each workshop would visit the counselor. In 1963,
four of us were experimenting with some ideas about
creativity and personal growth,[24] and it occurred to us
that there would be some advantage to omitting the
announcement of the use of a counselor. The director

cooperated, and to our surprise no one requested a counselor.

At the end of the workshop, I attempted to find out why, since the workshop was quite intense. After talking to many participants, I concluded that the reason they did not seek help was very much related to the expectation of the leaders. When we provided a counselor, we were conveying to the participants our belief that they were not able to deal with every contingency of the two-week period. When participants reached a stressful point, they obligingly assumed this was the moment where they needed help, as the leaders had implied they would. When no such announcement was made, the message conveyed to the group members was that the staff felt they would be able to deal with whatever situation arose. When they reached their stressful moment, they assumed that since the leaders assumed the group members could deal with it themselves, they could deal with it—and they did.

For me, this was extraordinary. It was contrary to my academic and psychoanalytically oriented training. It was inconsistent with the medical model. It was also very reasonable. If I, the group leader, expect you, the group member, to be weak, then I elicit the weak part of you. If I expect you to be able to cope, I elicit your strength.

Since that time, I have continued to explore the area of self-responsibility. I was influenced especially by the thoughts of Fritz Perls and of Werner Erhard and by those found in the Seth books.[25] As I worked with the idea and began to speak about it, I found that more and more people were coming to similar conclusions.

Having been through a parallel experience with the concept of interpersonal honesty, I have a feeling that the concept of choice is one whose time has come. The notion that all people choose their own lives seems to have originated in several places, largely independently. For example:

Axiom X: Only you have responsibility for your
own evolution.

—Arica[26]

You are god in your universe.
You caused.
You pretended not to cause it so that you could
play in it.
And you can remember you caused it any time
you want.

—Werner Erhard[27]

See each problem not as something that just
happened to you, or as just being the way you are,
but as: (1) something you decided to do, (2)
some way you decided to be, or (3) some way
you decided to see other people. In other words,
see your problem as a decision you have made.

—Harold Greenwald[28]

Only you yourself can be your liberator.

—Wilhelm Reich[29]

. . . it is oneself who determines in most instances
whether they (the events in one's own life) shall
or shall not continue to exist.

—Fritz Perls[30]

Even Shakespeare hinted at the concept in *The
Tempest:* "What's past is prologue; what's to come in
yours and my discharge."

Each version differs somewhat from the others.
What follows below is my own view of the matter.

I choose my whole life and I always have. I choose
my behavior, my feelings, my thoughts, my illnesses,
my body, my reactions, my spontaneity, my death.

Some of these choices I choose to be aware of and
some I choose not to be aware of. I usually choose
not to be aware of feelings I do not want to deal with,

of unacceptable thoughts, and of some causal relations between events.

What has been called the unconscious is demystified by this formulation. I choose that too. My unconscious is simply all of those things of which I choose not to be aware.

There are no accidents. Events occur because we choose them to occur. We are not always aware that we are choosing them.

Once we accept responsibility for choosing our lives, everything is different. We have the power. We decide. We are in control.

If I accept the concept of choice, I must alter my understanding of many key concepts in encounter and psychotherapy, concepts like group pressure, manipulation, using people, brainwashing, scapegoating, and mind-fucking. All these terms imply that something is being done to me when in fact I am allowing something to be done to me. I use these terms to blame others for what I do myself.

Suppose, for example, that I hold to a particular belief while I am a member of a group. To my chagrin, I find that everyone in the group disagrees with me. After a great deal of "ratpacking" and "coercion" and "laying trips on me," the group "breaks me down" and forces me to change my mind.

Back in the warmth of home, I find that I still feel as I originally did. I begin to realize what has been done to me. This group has brainwashed me! They pressured me into changing my mind! The leader irresponsibly took advantage of his authority and overwhelmed me!

If I choose, I may content myself with this explanation, and I may even become an indignant critic of the "tyranny of groups." I might even relate my experience to Chinese brainwashing and write a paper demanding that ethics committees suppress this alien behavior.

However, if I accept the choice principle, I would go further and recognize that *they* did not change my mind; *I* did. All they did was to say and do things.

*I* interpreted what they said and did as being group pressure. *I* assigned the leader his or her authority. *I* accepted the group's projections as applying to me. Group members may have intended that my mind be changed, but I had to collude with them to make it happen.

As I reach this realization, I gain self-insight and I profit from the experience. What is there about my lack of security, my lack of stability, my off-centeredness, my need to be accepted, that leads me to change my mind when I do not really think differently?

While exploring my own uncertainty, I realize that the group gave me a gift. They created circumstances I used to discover how certain and how secure I am in my belief, how important it is for me to be liked, how mindlessly resistant I am, or how weak I am in what I believe.

As a leader of therapy or encounter groups, my emphasis is not on limiting what you are allowed to do (don't project, don't interpret, don't analyze, don't scapegoat, don't criticize). I encourage you to say anything. The recipients of your comments then have the opportunity to use them to learn more about themselves.

Not only do groups not pressure me, but things do not frighten me. I may say I am afraid of a person, like yourself; or of a situation, like rejection; or of a thing, like spiders. But to be consistent with the choice point of view, I am not really afraid of those things out there, I am afraid of my inability to cope with you or with rejection or with spiders. As long as I see you as the cause of my fear, I spend my time trying to change, criticize, avoid, or destroy you. But once I see that my fear is in me, I can deal with my coping ability —a much more useful enterprise.

There is only one fear: the fear of not being able to cope—of my own uncopability.

Suppose I am afraid you will come into my office because "you talk all the time," "you take up my time," "I never get anything done when you're around," "you intrude upon my privacy." I dread seeing you come.

I dread your coming because I do not feel able to cope with you. As soon as I learn to ask you to leave when I do not want to have you around anymore, I no longer dread your approach. When I feel I can cope with you in that situation, I have no fear.

It is not necessary to believe the choice concept in order to explore its consequences. If you assume choice to be true, you have a chance to discover whether it is true. If you assume that much of life is accidental, you will never know if it is or not. What's to lose?

As I have come to accept the choice idea over the past twelve years, I ask myself: Why do I choose to believe it? At the age of eight, my favorite poem was William Ernest Henley's "Invictus." The part I especially liked was the well-known "I am the master of my fate, I am the captain of my soul." Apparently, either I had a strong desire at that age to feel that I chose everything, or I had an early intuition that the choice idea was true, or both.

I also loved puzzles. One of my heroes was Sherlock Holmes. I spent hours on crosswords and logical puzzles. I once stayed up all night flipping a coin 12,000 times to see if the normal curve was true. If I choose everything, and if there are no accidents, then life becomes a soluble puzzle. If many phenomena are accidental, there is nothing to figure out. I prefer the puzzle.

## UNAWARE

Although their meanings are virtually identical, I prefer to use the terms "aware" and "unaware" instead of "conscious" and "unconscious," because I think they are more descriptive and more precise. For literary ease, however, I shall use them interchangeably.

Not all choice is aware choice. Or, to put it more accurately, in some cases, I do not let myself know that I am the chooser. At an early age, I may have decided that it is too painful to be aware of, for example, a feeling that everyone thinks I am stupid (and, more basically, that I think I am stupid). Therefore, I block my feeling of stupidity.

One of the behaviors I display in order not to have to face my feeling of stupidity is competitiveness. I cheat in order to make my competitors look no better than I. I also do not let myself know that I cheat, because, if I do, then I may have to realize my feelings of stupidity. Cheating becomes an act I am choosing to do and which I am not letting myself be aware of.

Further, I may feel guilty about cheating and not let myself know about my feeling of guilt. This guilt leads me to cheat in such a way that I get caught and punished and thereby expiate the guilt. I feel very angry with the people who caught me, while without awareness I have arranged the whole event of being caught.

One of the primary objectives of encounter and therapy is to help you, the participant, become aware of which phenomena you are unaware. Once you become aware, decisions you make are subject to your will. "Will" is a term I shall use to refer to a choice made with awareness. If, in the above example, I realize that I felt guilty, then I can with awareness choose whether I want to cheat.

Making the unaware aware is very similar to the traditional psychoanalytic objective of making the unconscious conscious.


## EVALUATION

Throughout this approach, the categories of good-bad, right-wrong, moral-immoral, ethical-unethical, are not used. Attribution of these qualities to a particular behavior is also a matter of choice.

Something happens—a behavior, an interaction—and that is what happens. That is what *is*. If I choose to call that behavior right, or moral, or unethical, I have that choice. Perhaps a large number of us agree to call it the same thing. But it is only what it is. Our agreeing that it is wrong does not make it wrong; it just makes it an act we call wrong. If others choose to call that behavior right, they may make that choice.

After experiencing that behavior, I may choose to react by feeling guilty, jealous, joyous, angry, loving, hurt. Others may choose to react differently to the same event. Ordinarily, I think I have no choice about the way I feel or react to the event. It is more accurate to say that I am not letting myself be aware of the basis upon which I choose the feeling. If I allow myself to discover this basis, I may bring the choice to my awareness and change it if I wish.

Sandra came to a workshop recently and told me she felt guilty for attending. I asked her to act as though her guilt were another person and to speak to it.[31] Her guilt replied: "I am here because you left your children at home."

It was true that she had left them at home, but, she asked, what was the advantage to her of feeling guilty about it? She immediately thought of what her own mother would say. If Sandra did not feel guilty, what kind of mother would Sandra be? At least feeling guilty showed the concern a "proper" mother should feel.

When Sandra became aware of this, she also became aware that she did not really feel guilty about leaving the children. They were having a good time and she felt she was doing a good thing. She was now aware of all the factors and could choose whether she wanted to feel guilty. She chose not to.

Evaluating my own feelings as bad delays my finding out what that feeling is. If I fear not being a man, I may choose not to acknowledge my fear of many situations. If I feel that sexual lust is immoral, I may not let myself know I feel such lust in certain circumstances. If I feel that wishing personal harm to someone is wrong, I may not let myself know I harbor such feelings.

I sometimes react to my unawareness by becoming very condemning of those who have the same feelings I block out of my awareness. I may deal with denying my feelings of lust by joining the Legion of Decency where I may be righteous by censoring pornographic movies while at the same time satisfying my own unaware desires by spending long hours watching sexual hijinks.

The premature death of his wife, the mother of his three children, had left Howard very depressed. She had been dead two years, but he still had not come out of his grief. He felt her loss very deeply, he said, and could not seem to get beyond it. As work with Howard progressed, it became clear that he had strong guilt about any negative feelings he had toward his wife, and he vigorously denied them.

As with almost all cases of loss of a close person, Howard's true feelings were a mixture of sadness, loss, anger over being left, resentment at having to bring up the children alone, and relief at being freed of the tense part of their relationship. As he came to see that these feelings were all right, he was willing to let go of his guilt and examine the feelings he actually had toward her.

As long as he expended energy maintaining the lie that all his feelings toward his wife were positive, Howard's energy for living was minimal. He had to acknowledge his real feelings and to accept them before his vital energy returned. After this was accomplished, his eyes glistened, his breathing deepened, and a great weight was lifted from him.

## PARENTS

How far back does choice extend? Do children choose? Do infants? Do we choose our parents?

I chose everything in my life from the beginning.

One woman was regressed to age nine months and could remember how she controlled her mother by knowing when to laugh, when to cry, and when to get asthma so her mother would have to stay with her instead of going out for the evening. Research is emerging on how children condition their parents.

The question of choosing parents requires a metaphysical belief about what happened before sperm met ovum. The Western assumption is that they have never met before combining to produce a fetus, and that the choice of which particular sperm fertilizes the ovum is largely due to chance. This is a view very difficult to prove.

So is my belief difficult to prove. Closer to the Eastern view, I believe in reincarnation in this sense:

We are all essences. We select a body and we live out a lifetime. There are usually some unresolved aspects of each lifetime. Easterners call these unresolved aspects karma. The essence must deal with its karma in order to evolve to a higher level. To do so, essence selects parents, genes, chromosomes, DNA, which permit it to work on the resolution of those issues. In part, then, we chose our parents so that we can work out our unfinished areas of difficulty. Usually we have trouble with them, and that is the whole point.

We can reasonably blame no one for our lives. We choose it all from before the beginning. Once we accept that responsibility, we can then set to work to change our lives—if we choose to.

## OPTIONS

While my choices are always from among options, all options are not equally simple to realize. At this moment, I find it more difficult to alter my blood pressure than to lift my arm. The first requires greater knowledge, expertise, body awareness, and control than

I now allow myself to possess. A century ago, altering blood pressure was even more difficult to achieve. Even if I assume, as I do, that I have the ability to do anything, and that I am not letting myself know that I have that ability, it is still valuable to distinguish degrees of difficulty in achieving certain choices.

The world creates conditions that make some options easier. Selecting the option: "Stay dry outside during a rainstorm" requires abilities few people have allowed themselves to master.

When we interact, I create conditions under which you feel certain options are more available to you or are easier for you to select. If you choose to go to a movie and I choose to handcuff you to the radiator, it is likely that I am creating a more difficult situation for you than if I were to drive you to the theater. I create the conditions. You interpret what they are, and within them you choose among options.

If I create conditions in which you find it easy to select options you desire, then you will seek me out and you will probably like me. If I create conditions in which you find it difficult to select desirable options, then you will be less likely to seek me out and to like me.

I always have the choice of creating conditions I anticipate will make the attaining of your choices more or less difficult. Your reaction to me is partly determined by the conditions I create. If you find your choices are difficult to attain within the atmosphere I create, you will probably attempt to change the situation by (1) changing me; (2) changing your perception of the situation I create to be more compatible with your wishes; or (3) leaving the situation.

## SOCIETY

The social structure resulting from each person's being self-responsible provides the basis for the best possible society.

Suppose I start lying and cheating and reneging on my promises. Because choices are nonevaluative, this choice is legitimate behavior. I am choosing to be a liar, a cheat, and a welcher.

If I make this choice, I may find that very soon I have no friends, I have been sued, I have lost my job, and I have two black eyes as a result of the way people have chosen to respond to my behavior. Quite probably, I shall now reconsider my choice to lie, cheat, and renege, and make a different choice.

My change of behavior is not due to any consideration of you; nor do I change my behavior to be kind, ethical, or altruistic. I change so that I will elicit from you the kind of response I wish.

I may also change because I want to think of myself as an upright, reliable person. My concept of myself is a strong motivator for my behavior. Since I can be any kind of person I choose, I select the kind I like best.

My most exhilarating personal experience with this power of the self-concept occurred during the McCarthy era when I was a college student at UCLA, faced with the issue of signing the noncommunist loyalty oath. Since I was existing largely on my income as a teaching assistant, the issue tested the strength of my principles—principles which directed me to not sign the oath.

After a long, thoughtful discussion with my father, who felt that I was right in principle but that I would jeopardize my future if I did not sign, I went into a restaurant with some friends. We weighed the matter and it seemed logical to sign the oath and to continue to fight it "from the inside." I decided to sign.

As I walked out into the sunlight, I felt a dark, heavy cloud settling over me. My body, which I was just learning to listen to, was telling me that something was not right.

At that moment, my voice spoke to me: "This is not the kind of person I want to be. I don't want to compromise a principle for a practicality. I won't sign."

With that, the cloud lifted and I felt light and open. My body had spoken again.

That was the first time I realized clearly that my behavior was my choice. I could be any kind of person I wanted to be. That was the simple basis of my behavior. Dozen of reasons were available to support any position, but they were just reasons. My decision was based on what kind of person I chose to be.

The social structure arises from people making their own choices. There are no "shoulds" in this world. Moralistic dictates, such as "looking out for one another" or "considering others' feelings," are not required; they flow naturally in a society with the focus on personal choice.

If I decide I want a positive response from you, then I discover what situations I create that you like. This requires seeing you and knowing you.

All behavior comes from selfish or self-interested motives. This is not inherently "good" or "bad." It is simply what is.

The choice principle implies that social minorities are oppressed only if they allow themselves to be put in a position they call oppression. The paradox is that this apparently reactionary social attitude returns "power to the person." As long as members of the minority believe that whites (or men, or straights, or the establishment) have oppressed them for hundreds of years, the only time the oppression can stop is when the majority decides to stop oppressing the minority. When the minority acknowledges that it is oppressed because it has allowed itself to be, then oppression stops when the minority members decide to stop allowing it. They have the power.

In the liberation movements of the past decades, the minorities started to make real progress toward their own liberation when they acknowledged their own responsibility and chose to change the situation. "Black power" and "Black is beautiful" were signs of this change of attitude and of taking back power.

## COMPASSION

There is nothing inherent in my belief that you choose your life which requires me to lack compassion for you. Compassion is defined as a feeling of deep sympathy and sorrow for another who is stricken by suffering or misfortune accompanied by a strong desire to alleviate the pain or remove its cause. For me, feeling compassionate means feeling a desire to create conditions within which you choose to alleviate your own pain. Even if I wanted to, there is no way I am able to remove your pain. Your pain is your choice, and you are the only one who can choose not to experience it. I only create conditions within which you find it agreeable to change your feeling.

The amount of compassion I personally feel for you depends on how much I care for you as a person and on three factors I perceive in you: (1) whether you accept responsibility for yourself; (2) whether you are willing to solve your own problem; and (3) whether you have let yourself know how to alleviate your difficulty.

If you take responsibility for your own situation and are willing and able to improve it, you generally require no compassion. My feeling is closer to one of warmth and of admiration for your style of coping with your life.

When you accept responsibility for your situation, are willing to solve it, and have not let yourself know how to solve your own situation, I have great compassion for you. If I think I know a method for solving your problem, I choose to assume the role of teacher. This situation is very common when I am the leader of an encounter group. People indicate a willingness to deal with their difficulties. They simply have not acquired the knowledge or skills or techniques to bring their struggle to a successful conclusion. I choose to present relevant techniques and ideas to them as options for their consideration.

My compassion for such people is even greater when I too am unfamiliar with the methods required to deal with a problem. Bob, a close friend, developed leukemia several years ago. He felt he gave it to himself, and to correct his condition he tried all the methods of cure he knew, from traditional medicine to psychic healers. I found myself totally devoted to thinking about and working with Bob to devise new possibilities for him to experience. My feeling of empathy with and closeness to him could not have been more complete.

The next strongest amount of compassion I feel occurs when you acknowledge that you are choosing your condition and you choose not to correct it yourself. Working out your own solution to a problem is often a big job and you may choose to give your responsibility to someone else. Illness frequently presents this type of problem. You are aware that you gave yourself the illness, but you do not want to undertake the probing and exploration required to solve the difficulty.

In this situation, I typically feel a bond of human frailty. What the hell, taking an aspirin is sometimes easier than doing guided imagery or a gestalt exploration. At times, becoming enlightened is a drag. When it becomes too oppressive, I turn to endarkenment (see page 204).

When you do not accept responsibility for your own behavior, my compassion pales. Suppose, for reasons you have not let yourself know, you feel jealous around me and you do not accept that you are choosing to feel jealous. My response, depending on circumstances, varies among these three: (1) You are creating your own problem by choosing to feel jealous. To collude with you I must curtail my pleasure, which I refuse to do. (2) I accept for now that you do not choose to accept responsibility for your jealous feeling, but because I know the pain of jealousy, however it is created, I choose to make it easier for you to avoid that pain. I will eliminate the situations I create to which you react with jealousy. (3) I choose to help you explore the true causes of the pain you call jealousy. This can be done at the same time I do not change my behavior (choice one), or at the same time that I curtail the jealousy-eliciting behavior (choice two).

This third choice is closest to "being helpful," in that it does not simply eliminate the irritating situation. Rather, it attempts to remove the cause of the difficulty.

I have the least compassion for people who refuse to take responsibility for their own condition. If you choose to blame the world for your situation, I will usually attempt to create conditions within which you will change your view. If you refuse, my compassion diminishes.

Two factors prevent my compassion from dipping to zero. To the degree that I doubt my own theory, I stay with you. If you feel intense hurt and jealousy, or if you are very ill and are not taking responsibility for these situations, the part of me that is not sure of my beliefs treats you in the traditional, sympathetic way.

I also respond with compassion when I recognize your fear of entertaining the possibility of self-choice. For many people, this belief requires a reinterpretation of their entire lives, with the mistaken anticipation that much self-blame and guilt must be accepted. In fact, choosing is simply choosing. It is not inherently good or bad.


## HELPING

A close relative of mine contracted a serious disease of the nervous system. I spent time with him, exploring the possibility of his taking responsibility for the ailment, suggesting that this might be the key to understanding and eventually arresting the disease. He would not accept this notion, preferring to continue blaming those around him for their neglect and inefficiency. My options were either to reject him because he refused to do for himself what I felt he could do, or to accept his level of awareness and to help alleviate his pain at that level.

My decision was to do some things he found immediately gratifying at his level of awareness, like spending time with him and taking him to an acupuncturist. I did not, however, collude with his picture of himself as a helpless victim by agreeing with his blaming, or by doing for him those things which he was capable of doing for himself.

To be most helpful in this situation, I served as a delay. I provided a support my relative did not have at the moment. I supplied him temporarily until he resumed his wholeness.

This is a model for governing, teaching, and therapizing. I, the leader/teacher/therapist, supply temporary support. It is always temporary, and it is in the service of your taking over your own life.

This is also a model for "helping." You are choosing to function at a low level of awareness. You are not aware that you are choosing everything. You are not aware of all your options. To be helpful, I choose to create conditions within which you find it easy to become aware of those levels which you have blocked.

My approach as a helper is to set the stage and, stepwise, to do the least possible to clarify your awareness. The more I do, the less helpful I am, balanced by the fact that sometimes doing a little more will bring the awareness (see Transition, page 146).


## EMPATHY

A friend of mine cut her hand. Two feelings rose in me. The first: "You chose it. What's the payoff? You must have wanted to cut your hand." True. She did. Very likely she was not aware of the reason why.

With awareness, she would rather not have had a severed skin. My second feeling: "She hurts. Even though she chose it, she is now in pain." I responded by providing advice, fetching palliatives, waiting on her, or acting in ways that I felt would lead to her having less pain.

This is how choice and caring are reconciled. People do choose everything. They are responsible for themselves. They choose to be in pain, to be confused, to be in difficulty, to be unhappy. Typically, they do not let themselves know they are choosing. The way they are now is the amount of awareness they are choosing. I can choose to give support while they discover their self-responsibility.

Looking at my friend's hand, it did not seem quite appropriate to "help" her by asking why she chose to cut her hand. Helping her to reduce the discomfort and to create conditions for healing felt better. Perhaps later, if she wished to, we might explore why she chose to cut herself, but not during the pain.

The more you let yourself be aware, the more you behave as a unified organism, "get your act together," and experience joy. Unhappiness comes from unawareness. However, if that is what you now choose, I may choose to create conditions within which you ease your present state, or I may choose to make the present situation one that I think you will choose to find more difficult.

There are times, perhaps, when understanding is what you desire. There are other times when you wish simply to rest where you are and feel good at that intermediate point. "I know I'm making myself miserable, but just hold me anyway." I have the choice to respond to that request in any way I wish.

Probably the most successful human relations are those which function along these lines: If you are unhappy, I empathize and create conditions you find easy to enjoy. I comfort, I sympathize, I support. At the same time, after you have resumed equilibrium, I work to help you choose behavior that does not result in unhappiness.

## SELF-COMPASSION

The same principles apply to my compassion for myself. I accept that there are times when I am not aware of why I choose something and that I choose not to expend the effort to find out. Instead, I accept myself where I am and I make my present state more pleasant.

Choice does not require a dogged, exhaustive, constant exploration of self. It is all right to relax, to be dependent, to be irresponsible. In the long run, I will probably find out that the more I take over my own life through my awareness, the happier I will be. However, I may go at whatever pace I choose.

While writing this book, I gave myself an excellent opportunity to test my self-compassion and my degree of belief in these ideas of choice. I contracted an illness. I took responsibility for having given it to myself. My conflict was: Would I undertake to heal myself, or would I go to the doctor and have him "heal" me? Following is an account of what happened, written while it was happening.

I am in the midst of a raging infection in my eyes. The doctor calls it bilateral conjunctivitis. I have had it for about nine days. It has gotten worse over that time, not better. Why do I have it?

I have not been sick for years. Nothing more than a few colds over the last five or six years. Certainly nothing like this. Why? I have a thousand explanations: I felt phony writing all these theories about illness in a book that someone thinks is worth a large advance. Thousands of people are influenced by me. They will read what

I say and believe it as perhaps thousands have in the past. And it is possible that I do not know what I am talking about. I have so seldom been sick. How do I know that I would not rush to the doctors if I were really sick? If I were put to the test, could I really control my health?

Through the wonderful mechanism of this illness which I have developed in myself, I am providing an arena in which I may find answers to these questions. My life-style has been to rotate between theory and experience. At this time in my evolution, theory is far outstripping experience. Thus, conjuctivitis. . .

So far, the results are mixed. Apparently, I only partially believe myself. If I followed my own teachings, I would react to the illness by (1) fasting; (2) doing guided imagery regularly; (3) resting; (4) lying in the sun; (5) getting plenty of fresh air . . .

Instead I eat. There was little sunshine. I mainly stayed in bed. Finally, I went to the doctor, tempering my visit by hanging on to the intention of making all the final decisions myself . . .

After stumbling badly in acting on my beliefs, I began to right myself. I did two truth processes (imageries), cut down on eating, actually fasted one day, played handball once, and sat in the sun. The sulfa drops the doctor gave me failed, so I had a respite . . .

Unfortunately, all of the methods I tried also failed, so I am once more back at the doctor, hoping he will find the "right" drug to restore me to clear vision. He informs me that if I do not follow his directions, I may lose my sight. That lays it on the line for my beliefs.

I must acknowledge that I have not allowed myself sufficient awareness to cure this condition, or, possibly, that my whole theory is wrong, but I shall entertain this possibility only if all else fails.

I am now ready for my second visit with the doctor. . .

The only thing working at all is a sulfa-steroid solution that is supposed to speed recovery. I continue taking it, for I am getting better in fits and starts. My eyesight has been affected, and it is very annoying not to see well. I am now in Palm Springs, resting, lying in the sun, but, alas, I am not fasting. Sunning feels absolutely right, the thing I should have been doing. I feel I will recover on this regime. However, I note that I am not stopping the drops. . .

The sunshine worked wonders. It is my day of greatest improvement. I have stopped the drops. The illness is teaching me that I do not now fully believe I am able to heal myself. I also feel clearly that if a similar affliction were to occur, I am now ready to follow my own ideas more faithfully.

I could berate myself for not acting in a way consistent with my beliefs. This would parallel being intolerant of others who are not acting in terms of self-responsibility. I could also accept the tempo of my own evolution. I believe that I can heal myself, but I do not yet believe it fully; that is, I do not spontaneously act consistent with that belief.

I am self-compassionate to the degree that I accept my incomplete belief and support myself while struggling toward total belief. I am self-helpful to the extent that I keep in mind my ultimate goal of being self-responsible. If I support my incomplete belief too long, I am no longer aiding my own evolution.

## RAPE

The choice principle implies that a rape "victim" is choosing to be raped and that the rapist is choosing to rape. They collude to bring about the outcome.

This is an idea that irritates a strong, highly emotional, national movement to the contrary. I do not mean that rapees are responsible in the same sense that it is often asserted. I do not believe that "they get what they deserve," or anything punitive. I feel that in most cases the rapees have an unconscious wish to collude with the rapist to perform the act of rape. Many rapees would not make such a choice if they were fully aware.

This also does not imply that rapists should go unpunished. One of the chief purposes of our laws is to prevent collusions with unconscious desires in order to allow time for these desires to reach awareness. For that reason, society often uses laws to deter such collusions as rape, murder, and robbery, events most people would not choose to be the target of, if they had total awareness.

A friend of mine was raped when she was five years old. If ever the idea of choosing to be raped was absurd, it would be in such a situation. I asked her to open herself to the possibility that she chose the event, and to see if that orientation made any sense to her. After reflecting for two weeks, she wrote me the following account.

It is autumn. Somehow I am five years old. My name is Wendy again. Little. I am telling my dog everything will be all right. I decide to run away because my parents will come for me. That will make them want me this time. They will love me then. At first I worry about getting dirty—my shoes and socks. I have on a pink and yellow dress. My hair is long curls. I am little, but I am big enough to run away. I decide to run away because the people in my house are dead and I am dead. Maybe there is someone somewhere who will take me, want me. Somewhere else something will change everything. I head for where I've never been. I will take care of Blackie.

I walk on the dirt road. He runs around me and in front of me and sometimes in the grass. We will not get lost. We go past the orchard and over a bridge. My shoes are dirty. We walk and walk and there are a lot of trees, but I know we are not in the mountains yet. There is a stream and I try to cup water in my hands so Blackie can drink. Then I can't find him anywhere. I look and look and call for him. He doesn't come. He is so little, he's only a puppy, he needs me. Pretty soon I am lost and scared.

It is still day. There is a man out there. He comes toward me and I recognize him. I decide that he is the one who is going to change everything, it will happen now, I am going to be all right. I run to him and then back away because he is carrying two dead birds. He has a gun, but I am afraid of the birds. He talks to me and remembers my name is Wendy. I ask him if he's seen my dog. My dog is lost..

He puts his gun over his shoulder on the side he has the birds. He takes my hand (my hand, I want him to—my hand is acceptable now, my hand is good and not ugly). He tells me he thinks he knows where Blackie is. I choose to go with him. We walk through weeds. There are some old buildings—I remember them and am not lost anymore. He says Blackie is in there. I am deciding what is going to happen. The man grabs my hand hard and says I shouldn't go in by myself.

He pushes the door open and we go in and I can't see because he shut the door. Please open it . . . (But I do not want him to. He does not. I want us to be alone.) There are only cracks between boards where light comes in. I tell him I want to go. I tell him Blackie isn't there. Blackie will worry if I don't find him. I have to go now. (I do not want to go. He does not let me.)

He does not let me. He does not let me go. I am on the ground, the dirt ground. He is on top of me. He's breathing hard, hard on top of me. (There is one thing I have not known about—

the secret place between my legs. Nothing about
me has been acceptable—but now I must find out
that this part of me is wanted by someone.) I cry
and scream. He is too big. He hurts me very much.
(But I wanted this to happen. I chose this to happen because there must be something good about
me.)

I am crying. He tells me to stop and I do. I feel
blood on me—I don't know if it's mine or from
the birds. He tells me never to tell anyone, not
ever. (I make him tell me this because I knew I
wasn't supposed to let anyone touch me.) He tells
me what he will do to me if I ever tell. I am very
quiet, I am trying to disappear, but still . . . Even
though I say that I won't ever tell anyone, I make
him do it to me anyway. He holds me down and
takes the dead bird and puts part of it inside me
and then he puts it in my mouth. I start to choke,
I feel the feathers in my mouth, I feel the blood
in my throat. (And now this is all I have to remember—I deliberately and completely block
what I made happen—all I have to remember is
my terror of birds.)

But my body carries full remembering—my
constant tension. With this I stop all feeling. I can
"go away" and not feel anything at all. My body
developed an enormous ability to hang on; I reinforced that hanging on for my own survival.

I developed poor eyesight and wore glasses—
as if I didn't want to see people close to me. If I
could clearly see them, I'd see also that I was not
valued, was not important. I hid behind them,
had a strong resistance to getting the contacts I
now wear, not wanting to give up any protection.

My breathing shortened, my head bent forward,
my face cast downward all the time as if I could
not be exposed, could neither be seen nor have to
see anyone. Constant tension in my stomach, my
throat always tight, rarely talking, often fearful
of choking, deep shame about my body and about

myself, often feeling frozen and paralyzed into not moving, not making any noise.

Since childhood, I held on tighter and tighter —nasal passages blocked to further prevent breathing, extremely infrequent periods, and now a cyst has developed deep inside me.

The only "freeing" things that seem to be natural for me are the feelings that my hands are graceful and can do good things and a recent growing belief in the beauty of my body. The only completely natural act for me is sex. It is only in sex that my body is free of all blocks, that my breathing is full and deep. It is only then that I am completely present and unrestricted. There is no holding on anywhere in me. I'm free and uninhibited. It is during sex that my whole being is recharged, energy flows through me, and I am completely alive.

It makes sense that it's natural because I chose to find out what was acceptable to other people, what was desired and what I possessed, when I was five. I chose to be sexually entered as a little girl—because I needed to be special, needed to be loved.

Certainly, not all persons raped have the same feelings as Wendy; nor do her feelings imply that rapists are without responsibility for what happens. I am suggesting that if the emotionality of the event could be suspended so that we could explore what really happens in each rape case, we may be able to understand better what is involved, and to take more appropriate measures to alter the situation if that is what we wish to do.


## DEATH

Since I choose everything, it follows that I choose my illnesses and my death. Every illness is a person's reaction to a present life situation. Every death is a suicide.

Being ill has many rewards. I am relieved of responsibility, given sympathy, waited on, allowed to rest, and made allowances for.

In a longer perspective, a generally weak constitution allows me to demonstrate that I was right and that my parents were wrong about the way they brought me up.[32] "You see, parents, if only you had listened to me, I wouldn't be in this wretched state."

Few people are aware of their choice of how and when to die. Suicides are an obvious exception, and so are some more subtle dying procedures.

I was struck by the way Fritz Perls, founder of Gestalt Therapy, preceded his death. After he had succeeded in a lifelong ambition to establish a gestalt community, he went home to Europe to visit the places and people of his early years. Then he went to Florida to visit his lover, then to New York to see his wife. Having completed those activities, Fritz went to Chicago, became ill, let the doctors operate on him—a practice that was almost unheard of within Fritz's philosophy—and died. It appeared to me that Fritz said goodbye to the most meaningful parts of his life, then departed.

Some people may plan to die in twenty years, so they start smoking or acquiring other habits that will eventually do them in. The transactional analysis (TA) concept that people live out a life script[33] is consistent with this view. TA sometimes asks people to predict when and how they will die. Those people who subsequently expired were found to have been remarkably accurate.

If indeed we all have a plan for our own demise, bringing the plan to awareness would allow us to decide deliberately rather than to decide without letting ourselves know what we have planned.

My fear of airplanes, auto accidents, or earthquakes has diminished to nearly zero as I allow myself to be more and more aware. On a plane, I feel I am not choosing to die now, and read the paper instead.

This attitude is not the same as denial, that is, not

thinking about it. And it is not the same as trying to put it out of my mind. For me, denial is colluding with unawareness. I prefer to entertain the possibility, in this case that I may die on a plane, and to decide against it. Once that decision is made, assuming that I have full awareness, I need not remake it for each plane ride. I do check in occasionally to see that no new decisions have slipped in of which I am unaware.

Guilt over the death of another person is greatly alleviated when I accept the idea of choice. If people die because they choose to, feeling guilt over that person's death is irrelevant. Feeling responsible for another's death becomes an act of misguided arrogance. I not only did not cause the death, I am not capable of causing the death.

Clarity on choice of illness and death removes the value of those events for manipulating others. I only allow myself to be manipulated by someone who is ill, or threatens death, if I believe I have some responsibility for that person's illness or death. All I can do is to create conditions they choose to find easy to use to become ill or to die. They choose. As soon as I accept that, I am free to choose not to be manipulated.

My guilt often has at base my desire, either aware or unaware, for the death or dis-ease of others, not on their actual conditions. I may then collude with their unaware parts to make it easy for them to make themselves ill in a way they would not choose to if they had full awareness. My guilt is over my desire, not over their illnesses.


## CULPABILITY

If I go to a businessman, sign a contract, and get swindled, who is culpable? If a salesman tells me he will do one thing and does another, who is culpable?

We both are. I choose to be treated as I am, and you choose to treat me as you do. If our interaction is a collusion, then what is the role of punishment or blame?

If we both have total awareness, there is no need for laws. All acts are agreements between consenting humans. Laws, or the assignment of culpability, arise because we do not have total awareness. As mentioned above, the law exists, in part, to protect me from myself. It exists for those situations where I do something without awareness that I would not choose to do with awareness.

For example: Awarely, I want a good car and unawarely I want to be taken advantage of so that I may elicit sympathy and support. The dealer wants to make more money. He colludes with my unawareness. He does this by lying. I am taken in by the lie because I really want to be lied to, just as Wendy wanted to be told not to tell. My unawareness is communicated to the dealer.

When I am on trial, one of the functions of a jury is to balance my aware objection to the crime with my unaware desires to collude in the crime. The jury decides either that my unaware wish would be the same if it were an aware wish, or that my unaware wish would have been different if it had been an aware wish.

Assume that Patty Hearst, unawarely, wanted to be abducted and to participate in SLA activities, perhaps to express her rebellion to her family. The legal question may be stated: If she were to let herself become aware of this desire, would she still choose it, or would she change her mind? If the jury decided she would have chosen it awarely, then the abduction constituted no crime, consenting adults, the SLA and Patty Hearst, simply did what they wanted to do in this instance.

Patty Hearst is most culpable if her unawareness, when brought to awareness, would lead her still to rebel through cooperation with the SLA. She is less culpable if, with awareness, she would choose not to cooperate with the SLA. Here is the paradox.

Suppose the truth is that Patty wanted to rebel, that she let it be known that she was available to be used by a terrorist gang, was delighted at her kidnapping and very pleased to get into the fray as a revolutionary.

This was her major feeling, but let us assume she also had some conflict.

If she were fully aware, a jury would almost undoubtedly send her to jail. If she let herself be aware only of the side of her that did not want to cooperate with the SLA, she would have a good chance of being exonerated as an innocent victim. The paradox is that the law rewards unawareness.


## SPONTANEITY


My ex-wife and I were running groups together in Australia for about six weeks. For a while, it was pleasant to work together. Then I began to feel critical of her for the heinous crimes she had been committing, like not laughing consistently at my jokes, or squeezing the toothpaste from the middle. One morning, I woke up first. I was very angry and ready to tell her exactly how I felt, a good, healthy expression of feelings, right?

A voice leapt into my head: "Why are you choosing to be angry?" it said.

"Be quiet," said I. "I am expressing my feelings. She should hear it anyway for her own good."

"But you know you are choosing your anger. Why are you choosing to be angry?"

"Don't be ridiculous. My anger is a spontaneous feeling. You don't mean to tell me that even spontaneity is my choice?!"

She slept through all this. Another crime. I began to ruminate. Maybe my spontaneous anger *was* my choice. As I thought about it, the truth of that paradox became apparent. All that was necessary to reconcile the apparent contradiction between choice and spontaneity was to add the dimension of time.

At some time in the past, I apparently had decided that whenever someone squeezed a toothpaste tube in the middle or committed a comparable felony, I could engender guilt in them, or discourage them from repeating the act, or elicit sympathy from others, by becoming angry. This decision was put into my computer, that is, into my nervous system, and from that time forward I would react angrily whenever such crimes were perpetrated. In other words, I decided what my spontaneous feeling would be in the future.

I choose my spontaneity.

If I allow myself to learn how to reconsider my original decision, I can change that decision. Human potential techniques provide a wide variety of methods for recovering early decisions: imagery, psychodrama, gestalt, bioenergetics, truth processing, rebirthing, even psychoanalysis. They offer methods for changing what appears to be spontaneous behavior.

## LOCAL CONTROL

The concept of choice has implications for the relation between individual decision-making and outside intervention. When individual units, such as people or groups, come into relation with each other, a structure is often formed to regulate that relation. The choice principle sheds some light on the nature of that structure.

Small units run large units effectively only with the cooperation of the large units.

I once conducted a year-long encounter group for prison guards at a large California penal institution. After we had gotten to know each other well, the guards confided in me. One of their secrets was that there was no way they could run the prison without the assistance of the inmates. Their small groups of guards, even backed by authority, weapons and experience, were no match for the much larger group of inmates if the latter chose to rebel and resist. Later, a former long-term inmate extended this point. He claimed that the only reason the prisons run at all was that the innocent men among them, the unjustly convicted, provide the necessary stability.

The same holds for healing. There is no way a physician can deal successfully with the body without the body's cooperation. The best a physician can do is to get in harmony with the body and to support its healing processes and, occasionally, to delay the body from destroying or harming itself until it has time to mobilize its healing processes, as, for example, when a body is crushed in an automobile accident. In such a case, the patient ordinarily does not have enough body awareness to effect a total healing unaided. Surgery can set the bones and medication can retard infection so as to buy time for the natural healing processes to take over.

In a current approach to holistic medicine, this point is incorporated into the treatment philosophy.[34] Hospital care is divided into three parts, body care, transition, and patient integration. In the first phase, I, the patient, choose to give up most of my autonomy and allow you, the doctor, to minister to me. I authorize you to use your expertise to get me through the immediate crisis which I do not feel adequate to cope with. In the second phase, I gradually take over responsibility for my own care and use my bodymind for healing. The third phase focuses on my own learning through examining why and how I gave myself the illness and how I healed myself. Outside assistance is used as first aid only until I am mobilized to heal myself.

# SIMPLICITY

---

> Hence, every atom is a wholeness bearing within it the stamp and signature of the whole world, every grain of sand an image of the universe. . . . If the same signature be in all things, then it follows that one simple set of laws is applicable to the whole diversity of manifestations.
>
> —Manly Palmer Hall[35]

The concept of choice is very powerful. Implications of the concept are staggering. But the concept is unfinished. The yin, or receptive side, must be explored, and that leads to other important ideas . . . to the path, to naturalness, and to simplicity.

## THE YIN OF CHOICE

During the years that I have been thinking about the concept of choice, an uneasy feeling gradually made its way to my full awareness. At first it was a feeling of vague discomfort, then an irritant. Finally, I faced it. There is something incomplete about the concept of choice. Too many times when I was replying to critics of the concept, I cleared my throat, a sign that I was not sure that I knew the answer to their objections.

The process through which I am discovering the incompleteness is itself an illustration of what is missing from the concept of choice. During a tour through Australia recently I met one woman whom I found attractive, but she would not have me. We had one prolonged and pointless conversation, departed, and I sulked and forgot about her.

Six months later, I received a letter beginning, very accurately, "It's probably a surprise to you to receive this letter." At the end of the letter she made a comment that, instantly, I felt was right, long before I had a chance to think about it.

> I've been thinking that your God-within concept has truth but is essentially masculine (vertical) and I think it needs to be balanced by an appreciation of its unity and communality in all. Like humanity as a whole has its God, which is shared by all.

Jackie had reinforced the hidden uneasiness I had been feeling, brought it jarringly to my awareness, and provided me with a direction for finding the solution. I was delighted at the incongruity of the vehicle for getting me going, a totally unexpected letter from a forgotten, apparently unsuccessful relationship, originating, almost exactly, from the other side of the world.

The second source of inspiration was equally unlikely. I was watching the Merv Griffin Show. Merv had on a particularly lame singer-comedian who was about to tell one final joke. I listened, distractedly, only to hear the second startling clue.

He told of a man who had the good fortune to visit both heaven and hell. In hell, he found everyone sat around a table piled with delicious food, but their elbows would not bend and they had no way to get the food to their mouths. The inhabitants of hell had to spend eternity in this frustrated state. In heaven, the situation was exactly the same. "Well then, what is the difference between heaven and hell?" asked a friend. "The only difference," he replied, "is that in heaven they feed each other."

Tears came to my eyes. What a beautiful tale. What an unlikely source for hearing it. Again I felt, pre-logically, that this was a very important story and was directly connected to what Jackie had said.

From the other end of the world and from a pathetic comedian came what I was looking for. In order to choose to hear these messages I had to let myself be passive and available to what the universe was telling me. I had to lie down, be horizontal, and exhibit the very openness I was learning about.

## THE PATH

The yin side of choice recognizes the simplicity of the world and the reduction of options to a small number, ultimately one, when the world is perceived clearly. The yin or receptive orientation requires sensing the world such that the path to be chosen becomes obvious.

When a running back in football takes the ball and looks downfield, there is a path that will take him farthest with the least effort. The best runners sense this path and, as they move, they intuitively compute their series of speeds, the places to change direction, the use of their blockers, the times and methods to fake, the places for straight arm.

If they select a different path, they may still make yardage but the efforts of running over people and the dangers of injury are increased. This phenomenon might have been what the great football player Red Grange referred to when he replied to the question, "Why are you a great runner while others just as fast, just as shifty are only good runners?" "A sense of the dramatic," was his response.

In the Japanese art of Aikido, the warrior is taught to blend with his attacker, not to oppose him. The Aikido master uses the simplest movement to utilize the power already exerted by his adversary. There is an exact spot to apply that pressure and a precise movement that will subdue the opponent. In con-

trast are the Western arts of boxing and wrestling
which are characterized by force overcoming force.

Eating good food aids health. So does breathing clean
air, being exposed to sunshine, and exercising. These
activities lead to health in the simplest and most direct
way. They are not, however, necessary to good health.
It is possible, given great self-awareness, to be healthy
despite the lack of these experiences, just as it is
possible to make a touchdown by running over people.

The same is true for astrology and biorhythms. Assuming that they are accurate, they simply indicate
which propensities are simpler for you. You may also
contravene them and accomplish what you wish. You
simply have to work harder and be more aware.

For any given situation, there is the simplest path.
Awareness reveals the path. The ultimate simplicity is
to choose the correct path. Teaching consists of creating conditions that help students find their own paths.

It is not always desirable to take the easiest path.
Since joy comes from using your potential, if the easy
path has already been accomplished, you might have
more opportunity to use your other potentials by trying
a somewhat more difficult route.

This does not imply pain. It is very likely that if
new paths are taken a step at a time, each path a bit
more difficult than the last, pain and discomfort may be
avoided entirely. Growth does not require pain.

## CHILDREN

When a child is perceived as unfolding on its path
several traditional problems fade, such as birthing,
feeding, and discipline. With the advent of Grantly
Dick-Read, Lamaze, and Leboyer,[36] childbirth, once
regarded as one of the most painful and unpleasant of
human experiences, is becoming one of the most beautiful and ecstatic. By harmonizing with natural energy,
rather than anticipating terrible pain, natural child-

birth perceives the experience of birthing as a wonderful
natural process to be approached without fear and to
be created into the most enjoyable situation for mother,
child, father, and all involved.

Leboyer describes a method for allowing the child's
entry into the world to be warm, quiet, close, and loving. The mother finds the natural tools she has available
for birthing, primarily relaxation and breathing, to flow
with nature. The position for birthing is dictated by the
mother's comfort and by her body's relation to gravity.
Aspects of birthing developed for the doctors' con-
venience (such as strapping down the laboring mother,
forcing her to lie on her back, and administering drugs
that contaminate not only the mother but also her
child) are being left in the wake of the return to the
natural, simple method.

Sometimes our rush forces us into trying to push the
river. No need. As Alice Bailey said, "There is no such
thing as failure; there can only be loss of time."

When Ari was about six months old his mother took
him to visit her parents. They were concerned about
him. He was not fat like the other children. At that age,
he was being breastfed almost exclusively. When I
learned of the grandparents' concern, I started to think
about the problem. When do you give a child solid
food?

I consulted several baby books, asked doctor friends,
and received many answers: four months, one month,
eight months. That did not seem to help. Perhaps I
should study biochemistry to see what ingredients were
omitted from Ari's diet.

All of this started sounding very complicated. I then
called upon a man I had come to respect in the nutrition
area, Herbert Shelton.[37] By observing the animals on the
farm where he had been brought up, Shelton derived his
principles of nutrition. Children should be given solid
food, said Shelton, when they have teeth.

How wonderful. Of course. A profound simplicity. It
turns out that the enzymes needed to digest solid food
are produced when teeth arrive. As I watched Ari, I

noticed that he started indicating a desire for solid food at just about the time his first teeth appeared.

If I had just focused on the masculine part of choice I may not have let myself be open to the natural solution for the question of solid food initiation.

Child discipline is subject to the same considerations. Ari is now in the so-called "terrible twos," a description of two-year-old behavior that I find curious, since discipline problems with Ari may be almost non-existent. They arise only when I stop progress on his path—if I want him to go to bed when he is not tired, to put on his clothes when he wants to be free of them, or to wipe his nose when he is playing and cares nothing about how he appears to the neighbors. If I become sensitive to his unfolding, discipline is minimal.

This does not mean that he does everything he wants. When he hits me in the face, I tell him sternly to stop or to make it nice. He usually tries it once or twice to make sure he has the message, then he stops. The more I avoid stopping him for unnecessary reasons, the more he complies when I do stop him.

When I regard him as the enemy, as someone who pushes the limits to see how much he can "get away" with, I have trouble. When I regard him as someone trying to get what he wants and to have a good time with me, magical things happen.

Looking at him from this perspective, I saw that when he walked into the street, he was really asking a question, not challenging me. One day I told him to stay out of the street. Next day I carried him when we crossed the street. Occasionally, when there was no traffic, I held his hand while he crossed. On isolated roads, I would even let him go across alone while I walked alongside. Now he was asking, "What are the rules? How do I generalize? When is it all right to walk in the street and when isn't it?" As I get clear, and as he understands, he complies. He enjoys complying. He derives a great deal of satisfaction out of mastering the road-crossing situation. We are both seeking the same goal.

There is a path for each child in his or her own unfoldment, and for unfolding with other people. When these paths are recognized, complied with, and chosen, what follows is less conflict and more joy.


## FLOW

Several years ago, my wife and I decided to move from Big Sur to be nearer San Francisco so we could apply to the establishment what we had learned in the human potential experience. We wanted the Big Sur atmosphere combined with easy access to the city— no small requirement. Investigation of the San Francisco Bay area led us to conclude that Muir Beach was the closest place to fulfilling our desires. And there, we felt, the problem began. Muir Beach is a very small community, forever limited in size by the surrounding national park, with precious few available building sites or houses for sale.

Gallantly, we prepared ourselves to visit several realtors, to tell our friends to put up notices, and to walk the area. Just as we were digging in for the long, hard search, a friend came by. "I just bought a piece of land in Muir Beach that I'm not going to use. You're welcome to it at the price I paid."

(That's nice, thought I, but it is probably not what we want.)

We went to Muir Beach, prepared to spend days, perhaps weeks, searching. Within the first day it became clear that our friend owned the very best piece of land available. Then we met a man who lived across the street from the property. "I love to build houses in Muir Beach. Be happy to build yours."

(Probably not a very experienced builder, I mused. I will certainly have have to explore further.)

Casual talk with our friend Marilyn, a resident of Muir Beach, added another element. "Oh, you are interested in Al's land. Did you know that Jerry, an old boyfriend of mine, a fine architect, already designed a house for that site? I happen to have a set of the plans right here."

(What good are plans designed for someone else, I grumbled.)

I was stunned as we looked at them. Except for being far more esthetic, they looked almost exactly the way we had sketched out our own house.

I called the architect the next day. He just "happened" to have made a model of that house, which was available. And he was a humanistic architect, interested in the relation of people to space.

For the first time, I dropped my cynicism and started to pay attention to the flow of events. Up to now, I had been setting aside everything that was happening to us, in preparation for my ordeal with the realtors. When I let myself experience the events, when I stopped trying and let myself go with the flow, everything was simple.

With no strain on our part, we had been offered a choice piece of land, a builder, an architect, and an ideal building design for which all the hard-to-get permits had already been granted. Apparently, we were ready for this house.

Right after that decision the energy flow changed. We decided to get a bank loan and build. The bank turned me down. Now that I was listening to messages, I took it to mean that the house was right, but that I needed more money before starting. I took two jobs and three months later applied to another bank, received the loan, and the house is now completed.

This experience is similar to an event that occurred in a Feldenkrais class. Moshe Feldenkrais was doing body manipulation on a woman who had been divorced about a year. During that year, she had been unwilling to deal with her feelings of grief over the separation; she felt stuck in her life. Suddenly she began to cry and continued for about twenty minutes. Feldenkrais's manipulation had freed the tension she was feeling, and she was finally able to express her buried feelings. Afterward, she looked light and relaxed and we all felt wonderful. However, Feldenkrais was sitting in a corner, looking gloomy.

"What's the matter, Moshe? You have helped Elaine do a very valuable thing. Why are you so sad?"

"Nonsense," he said. "I went too fast. If I had done it properly, she would not have had to go through the crying. She would have released normally, within her capacity to handle the feeling."

I was mystified. My professional experience had led me to feel that her crying was ideal, a much-needed release of pent-up feeling. But I had so much respect for Moshe that I began to reflect on his idea. Perhaps he was right. Perhaps there *is* learning without pain.

His approach to exercise assumes that if we understand our bodies well enough, we can have them do whatever we want them to do without subjecting them to strain. It requires more self-sensitivity and awareness. I have a suspicion that Feldenkrais is in touch with a deeper truth.

## THE SIMPLE

Recognition of paths implies that, at bottom, the universe is simple. When we apprehend what is, it is simple. Complexities that require an involved process of choice dissolve and choices are obvious.

I assume that there is a simple order in the world. Human beings started simply, from one cell, from one common pair of parents, and from that simple beginning we multiplied and interrelated. As we unravel our mysteries, we retrace our evolutionary steps back through complexity to simplicity.

When I look over the books I have written, I know exactly which parts I understood and which parts I did not understand when I wrote them. The poorly understood parts sound scientific. When I barely understood something, I kept it in scientific jargon. When

I really comprehended it, I was able to explain it to anyone in language they understood.

Any complex explanation is an intermediate one. It always struck me as absurd that I must become a biochemist to know what to eat; that a woman must be drugged and manacled to have a child; that it takes millions of dollars to collect taxes equitably; or that life's major decisions are determined by coincidence.

I assume that I give a complex answer to a question because I do not understand the answer at a very profound level. To a truly profound explanation, everyone should reply: "Of course." Each person should already have the confirming evidence in his or her own experience. The discoverer has only the advantage of formulating it in a way that everyone can recognize, in the manner of a good humorist or of a good artist.

Understanding evolves through three phases: simplistic, complex, and profoundly simple. When I first approach an area of interest, I find it very simple and very obvious, and I am more than a little mystified that everyone is so puzzled. I was that way when I entered my first encounter group.[38] At that time, I believed an encounter group consisted of a bunch of people sitting around expressing their feelings. I could not understand why the group members spent so much time making decisions. It took them three meetings to decide whether to let me in the group. I expressed exasperation: "Why do you anguish so long? It's so simple. Take a vote. Yes or no!"

Gradually, it became clear to me that something else was happening in the group, something beyond counting votes. People were expressing feelings. This was a world to which I had never paid much attention. I began to see what an encounter group really was and, in particular, how wonderfully complex it was.

In addition to learning the mechanics of groups (they usually consist of from eight to thirty people who are usually sitting on cushions) I discerned their dynamics. Group members are there to learn how to allow themselves to assume responsibility for their own lives and to learn how to be honest and aware of themselves so as to avoid self-deception. As I watched I saw that these aims were accomplished by telling the truth, by paying attention to the body and to the signals coming from it, by getting in touch with and expressing feelings, by relating primarily in the here and now, and by risking behaviors the participants found difficult. As people did these things, I saw them unblock their energies and allow themselves to flow more freely with living.

Understanding the group process suddenly became very complicated. Many, many factors had to be taken into consideration in order to understand group phenomena—psychological, sociological, historical, familial. My understanding of the group went from simplistic to complex. I spent many hours explaining that we must take all factors into account, that we must consider all the variables.

The next stage of understanding returns to the simple, but at a deeper level. Order lies beneath complexity. My efforts at ordering group phenomena resulted in the hypothesis that all group behavior may be understood as variations around three interpersonal needs: inclusion, control, and affection (see page 111). Group behavior simple again.

A powerful example of profound simplicity, the one that awakened me to the concept, is in the 1912 work of Bertrand Russell and Alfred North Whitehead, *Principia Mathematica*.[39] In that book, the authors considered the enormous complexity of mathematics and demonstrated that it could be reduced to five simple, logical operations. From these operations all mathematics could be derived.[40] I remember responding to their work with enormous excitement while noting how odd it was to feel so emotional about an intellectual achievement.

Fueled by the Freudian revolution, the field of human behavior has passed through the appreciation-of-complexity phase and is now prepared to enter the phase of profound simplicity. I am not presuming that this book completely maps the profound simplicity phase. My intent is to point to some directions for finding the basic elements.

## UNITY OF LAWS

It is inelegant that the principles of group behavior should be different from those of individual behavior, or the body, or social institutions, or nations. God doesn't play dice with the universe, Einstein assumed. Why should science be so complicated? Why should scientific terminology be so esoteric? If something is true, should it not be simple enough to be understood by anyone?

I assume that the same laws hold for all levels of social and biological organization. The laws consist of characteristics of the elements at that level—atom, cell, organ, person, couple, group, nation, planet, solar system—and of the rules for combining these elements. As above, so below.

The fact that concepts are parallel provides a powerful tool for understanding human organization. As soon as something is discovered on one level, it can be applied to all other levels.

In a small group experiment many years ago, I devised a technique to demonstrate the parallel between phenomena on the levels of group and individual. I asked people in a small group to make a decision about something currently important in their lives—whether they should get married, change jobs, move, go back to school, have a child, or whatever. They were to note the content of their decisions as well as how clear or how conflicted those decisions were. Then I asked each person to think of five or six people who had had the most influence on their lives—parents, siblings, teacher, childhood hero, friend—and to imagine those people having a discussion among themselves about the same issue.

Striking similarities both in the content and in the certainty of the decision were revealed when the decision made by the group of introjects was compared to the decision made by the person alone. Each person behaves on the basis of a group inside the head. The influence of a synthesis of introjected people pervades each individual's behavior.

I suspect that eventually we will find that another reason for this parallel is that there is consciousness at all levels of existence and that each level of organization operates as a being. The existence of small, apparently independent worlds within the mitochondria of our cells[41] points in that direction.

My personal, nonscientific belief in awareness at all levels was aided immeasurably by a psychedelic experience. I was virtually the only person on a small island in Tahiti. I had taken MDA, a chemical that sharpens the senses and brings the here and now into great clarity. As I looked down at the sand and the rocks and the sand crabs, within each of them I saw little stick figures waving at me as if to say: "Hello there, nice to see you, brother. Yes, we're here too." It was charming and very familiar, like a *déjà vu* experience I remembered from a time vastly earlier in my existence.

## NATURALNESS

Profound simplicity puts great faith in natural processes—the simplicity of foods, the healing power of the body, the natural evolution of interpersonal relations. It looks for answers in the earth, the sky, the trees, the animals, and in the human organism. These are the simple origins. They should reveal the simple solutions.

Several human potential techniques illustrate this principle very well.

In the Feldenkrais technique, the body is brought

along at its own natural speed so that increased flexibility and coordination occur without strain.

In fasting,[42] the body heals itself at its own natural pace, without the need for outside intervention.

In encounter, if the group is conducted properly, people do their work when they are ready. There is no need for force. If something is not happening smoothly, this means that the external situation is not yet ready to support it.

In mental imagery, the person goes directly to the picture that is relevant to the most salient issue.

## FASTING

About five years ago, I read a book with the modest title: *Fasting Can Save Your Life* by Herbert Shelton.[42] It made a deep impression on me. Four years later, I was driving along the highway and a thought went through my mind: "It's time to fast." I had been feeling thick and sluggish and fuzzy, and now a fast seemed just right. I looked up Shelton, found he had a health school in San Antonio, and I went down there and fasted, water only, for thirty-four days. The experience far exceeded the actual fast. I learned much more about following natural energy.

The health school was run along the principles of the Natural Hygiene group,[43] which has been in existence for over a hundred years. The part of their philosophy that attracted me related to the healing of the body. This group feels that the body heals itself. Outside agents, such as drugs, simply suppress symptoms and provide the body with another, mostly unusable, substance which it must expend energy to handle.

When I fast, they claim, my body nourishes itself by living off its reserves. Because it naturally goes toward self-preservation, the body uses first those substances which it needs least, namely, toxins, inflam-

mations, tumors, and the excess fat tissue where much
of the toxin is stored. The body then uses up, in order,
muscle, bone, and nerve tissue. Fortunately, when it
moves from using toxins and fat to using muscle tissue,
that is, when the body moves from fasting to starving,
it sends a clear signal. The signs of toxin removal—
body odor, bad breath, strong urine, coated tongue—
disappear and a strong, "true" hunger appears. At this
time, it is wise to eat, otherwise fasting becomes starva-
tion. This point is reached after different lengths of
fasting for different people, usually taking an average
of about forty days.

The absolute simplicity and naturalness of this
philosophy held great appeal for me and obviously
fit in with the natural philosophy at other levels of
human organization. Encounter encourages naturalness at the interpersonal level; Feldenkrais assumes it
for the nervous system; and fasting uses the same
principle for the body's physiology.

Belief in simple and universal laws depends on the
existence of an underlying bodymind unity. One level
is not yet accounted for: the intrapsychic, or personal,
level.


## IMAGERY


Belief in simple and universal laws depends on the
existence of an underlying bodymind unity.

The natural entry into understanding the intrapsychic, or personal, level is provided by the technique
called guided imagery.[13] Although devised in a
psychotherapeutic context, like most such techniques
it has a much broader application.

When doing imagery, you let a particular picture
come into your head. Traditionally, I, as the guide,
start you off with some symbol, like a cave, mountain,
sword, or photograph album. You then report what you
see, and I guide you through any travail you might

encounter. It is a most remarkable technique that leads to amazingly effective results.

Working with this method over the years, I have found that I use fewer and fewer initial directions, finally settling on: "Let a picture come into your head." I found that the less structured the instruction, the more likely it was that the imagery went straight to the place of most psychological difficulty. The body-mind knows where it has to go to work out a problem, in much the same way that in fasting the body knows what to rid itself of. In both cases, it is a matter of removing interference from the outside so that the organism itself has a maximum opportunity to do what it needs to do in order to optimize its own being. This parallels the definition of the purpose of democracy given by Reich (see page 170): to remove obstacles to self-determination.

## TEACHING

Parents are teachers. So are therapists, bosses, priests, physicians, coaches—anyone in a superordinate position. A good teacher creates conditions under which the students choose to find it easier to find their path.

Several months ago I visited Bhagwan Shree Rajneesh at his Ashram (school) in Poona, India. Rajneesh fascinated me. I had read many of his writings,[44] and they were brilliant. Many of my friends had gone to Poona and become sannyasins (disciples) of Bhagwan. I wanted to know what he was about.

The entire ashram was run along lines totally counter to those that I had espoused for years. To be a sannyasin I had to surrender to Bhagwan. I had to accept everything he said, to do what he told me to do, and never to question his authority. Vile! Where was the development of the self that I had been championing for decades? How could this fascistic approach reap a harvest of human unfoldment?

When I arrived at the ashram my first impression was that of Shangri-La. People walked arm-in-arm, they sang, they danced. There was a lightness about the place that I envied and admired. As I stayed longer, observed more and spoke at great length to the residents of the ashram, I heard more and more the word "channel." Everyone there was a channel for Bhagwan. Each person was a receptive conduit through which Bhagwan spoke. Ashram leaders felt no responsibility for any of their actions as leaders. They simply carried out the wishes of Rajneesh. Lightness seemed to follow the shedding of responsibility.

I left Poona with head swimming.[45] Everything I had been teaching was violated, yet there seemed to be great benefit occurring. How could this be? Surely I had not been wrong all this time.

Maybe, Bhagwan was developing, in a very powerful way, the yin side of choice. Surrender to Bhagwan, it was said, was simply a surrender to oneself. The critical, worried, anxious parts are surrendered. Sannyasins simply allow themselves to flow with what is. Perhaps Bhagwan was demonstrating that when a person is entirely open and receptive, choice is obvious. It was a disturbing and intriguing thought.

## COMMUNITY

With a few dramatic exceptions, we have all chosen to live in a society. We were not created in isolation. We issued from a mother and emerged on a peopled planet. A great deal of our gratification derives from being in relation to people. Existence without cooperation is extraordinarily difficult and rarely sought.

Like the parts of our bodies, the various elements of a social group often work in opposition to each other. When the elements of a system are each working up to their comfortable capacity—that is, functioning to their fullest without strain—and when all elements are being directed, or are self-directed, with such a sequence and timing that their overall objective is being accomplished optimally, the system is working to its capacity. At that point, it will naturally follow its path.

A paradox arises at this point, illustrated by China since the revolution. The Chinese philosophy is totally nonindividualistic. Everything is done "for the revolution," for the group or community in which each member is a sub-unit. Yet reports from China frequently note the curious phenomenon that the Chinese people seem to have self-confidence and self-acceptance, in a place where individualism is all but ignored.

Perhaps it works this way. I may choose to live alone, to retire to the jungle and provide my own food and shelter. Or, I may choose to live with other people so that I may eat without spending all of my time gathering food, or drive a car without building it myself, or experience myself more fully through interaction with another person.

With that choice, part of realizing my potential involves relating my optimal being to those of the people with whom I am in contact. Joy comes not only from realizing all the potential within myself, but also from the potential to become a part of a larger whole. Part of my joy comes from actualizing and coordinating all the elements inside myself, and part comes from integrating myself into a larger system.

The Chinese peasant may be feeling the joy that derives from relating well to other elements of a system, just as ball players often feel that team winning is more important than individual records. The object of playing on a team is to do what is required for that team to achieve its goal. Individual excellence is defined in terms of its contribution to that goal. That is why meditation does not lead to love, or love to personal optimal function (although each may aid the other, that is, if you learn how to cooperate internally you also may know how to cooperate externally, and vice-versa).

Perhaps a reason that many people are not happier is that they are not connected with a larger group. They are not employed in a regular job or are not members of an organization in such a way that their potential for blending themselves with others has not been developed. What is missing may not be the continual work to develop and integrate themselves internally. If they are not in a marital relation nor in a full-time work setting, they are not evolving as an element of a larger system.

Missing, too, is the part of themselves they learn by being in relation to others. The use of fitting with another person, or with a group, to provide insight into their own internal integration, is not there. How they deal with hurt, neglect, competition, love, jealousy, incompetence, and the other feelings issuing from being in relationship are not available.

Community provides the source of joy that derives from integration with others. It involves discovering and choosing the social path.


## YIN AND YANG OF CHOICE

The principle of choice describes the reality that I am in charge of my life. I choose it all, I always have, I always will.

Because, at bottom, the world is simple, there are paths in the universe, a natural flow that makes my choice, simple and obvious.

I discover these natural paths when I am open and receptive, when I sense what is inside and what is outside my body.

As you and I acknowledge our self-responsibility and as we open ourselves to the paths, we flow together. Our paths are harmonious and we create a joyful community and society.

# TRUTH

And ye shall know the truth, and the truth shall
make you free.

—John 8:32

In virtually all the psychological and spiritual
attempts to discover the divine, the concept of truth is
central. Truth allows me to continue the unfolding of
my evolution; it allows me to know what is happening, to
see what is.

Lying is a drag, literally. When I lie, I tie up my
energy in unproductive and largely unpleasant ways.
I tighten my body, contaminate my relations with
people, and become depressed and anxious. I constrict
my experience and eventually turn my life to tasteless-
ness.

The truth really does make you free, and honesty
really is the best policy. We have espoused these truths
for centuries, but most of us do not believe them for an
instant. We make our way through this contradiction
by inventing euphemisms for lying, words and phrases
such as tact, diplomacy, white lies, "business is business," and "let's be realistic." We establish an entire
field to encourage lying. It is called manners and
protocol, which says: "Act in the prescribed way
whether it is your true feeling or not." We even justify
lying with a bit of moralizing: "Don't hurt other
people's feelings." All these terms are forms for saying: "Lying is the desirable form of communication."

The breakthrough in this area is twofold. First, we
are now realizing that many old clichés are absolutely

correct. The truth does make you free—organizational-ly, interpersonally, personally, and in the body. Second, we now have the tools and techniques for finding what is true—specifically, feedback and body understanding —for testing the outcomes of honesty and for becom-ing more aware. We may proceed to turn these tools into action.

I will be more precise about my use of the terms.

*Truth* is what is, whether we know it or not. My truth is what is true of me, my experience, the state of every cell, of every atom, of my body, my memories, my thoughts, my feelings, my sensations.

How much I let myself know of my own truth is my *awareness*. Some things about myself I am afraid of, or ashamed of, or I feel guilty about. Those may be the things which I choose not to let myself know about.

That truth which I do not choose to let myself know about has been called my unconscious. Bringing that of which I am not aware to my awareness is the objective of many techniques in the human potential field and is the key to the joyful life.

If I choose to tell you of what I am aware, I am being *honest*. If I choose to tell you something con-trary to my awareness, I am lying. If I choose not to tell you something of which I am aware, I am with-holding.

To communicate my truth to you, I must be both aware and honest.

To be honest and not aware is what may be called the Gerald Ford (or Eisenhower) syndrome. When people are sincerely honest but have not allowed them-selves much self-awareness, what comes out is usually boring. They do not present themselves fully.

To be aware and not honest is the Machiavelli syn-drome. Such people are aware of their truth and choose to be deliberately deceptive.

## HONESTY

Suppose I am having an affair with my neighbor and do not tell my wife "for her own good" (a reason almost universally false). As I approach my home following a tryst in the country, I notice that my body tightens and I start to feel heavier. A light dread enters my awareness. "Must remember where I told her I was going. . . . Did I check with Gus to verify my story? . . . Any perfume smell?"

She greets me lovingly at the door. (Why does she have to be so nice!) "Hello, darling, how was your day?"

"How many times do I have to tell you I don't want to have to report to you everything I do. If a marriage is going to work, people have to get away from each other once in a while. A man's work should be separate from his homelife." (Think I'll write an article about that!)

After a supper of artfully not saying a great deal and of being overwhelmingly absorbed by the newspaper, I go into the living room to relax. I am very tired and very tense, curiously much more tense than when I am not in the house.

"There's a wonderful show on television tonight, dear. Would you like to see it? It's about adultery."

"No! . . . Er . . . I'd rather see something light. Is the ball game on? Anyway, I feel tired. Think I'll go to bed early." (I'm really exhausted. Maybe I'm getting sick, or old.)

"The Ralstons asked if we could visit them tonight. I think they're having some troubles."

"No."

And on it goes. The more interaction I have, the more exhausted I become. My muscles tighten, my patience drains, and our relationship becomes very unpleasant. If I do not have insight into what is happening, I am only aware that my marriage is getting dull.

We never talk about anything anymore. Of course we don't. I do not allow it.

What I have given up, primarily, is my spontaneity. I cannot afford to be spontaneous because my secret may be revealed. The price I pay for curbing my spontaneity is measurable by the loss of energy and by the deterioration of our relationship. I am physically exhausted because lying, either deliberately or through withholding, requires a great amount of physical and mental energy. That becomes clear when the boys call up later in the evening and I find myself bowling till two in the morning, full of energy.

My marriage deteriorates mainly because I am holding back a large part of myself. Not only do I not tell about my dalliance, but I do not allow myself to explore either the difficulties in my marriage or the feelings I am harboring about my wife, which I use to keep from getting closer to her.

Dishonesty holds me back, blocks me, stops my flow, ties up my energy, and exhausts me.

Communication of truth makes for interpersonal richness. To really meet, to fully present ourselves to each other, and to have the most satisfying human relations, we must be both aware and honest.

This is certainly true in a marriage where full openness to each other may lead to acceptance of the mates as they really are, not just acceptance of the image they are projecting.

Objection is frequently raised to this conception of honesty. If I really told my boss the truth, it runs, I would be fired. "The truth" usually means outrage, name calling, anger, and criticism.

The problem ordinarily is not that there is too much honesty, but rather that there is too little. Anger and criticism are indeed true feelings, but they are usually reactions to a prior feeling. The deeper feeling may be: "I feel hurt when I don't feel appreciated by you," or "I feel depressed because I feel you don't like me." If *these* feelings are communicated honestly, occupational demise is much less likely.

I still have difficulty (that is, I choose to) believing in honesty, despite the fact that I "know" it is right. (I know it with my head.) Early in my house-building adventure, it appeared to me that I would "have" to be dishonest about an outstanding personal loan if I were to get a bank loan to build a house. Finding this out, I began scheming not to tell the bank about the personal loan. Then my daughter Laurie reminded me of the volumes I have writen about truth. "Yes, yes, but this is important!" But she prevailed. So I tell the bank the whole truth. Why do I tell them? Because I know it will be better to be honest. The worst that can happen is that I will not get the loan. Then what? Something else will happen. And, certainly, I will feel better. (I got the loan.)

## HYPOCRISY AND PRIVACY

Failure to believe our own adages leads to dreadful hypocrisy, sometimes as a national policy.

This duplicity reaches a fine art in legalisms. "Mr. Press Secretary, why didn't you tell us that . . . ?"

"Nobody asked me that exact question."

Withholding and omitting are sophisticated ways of lying. In the legal system, a lie is not really a lie unless you can *prove* it is a lie.

We try to inculcate this ethic into our children at a very young age. I took my son Ethan to the playground when he was about six, and we saw a typical scene. A little girl was being admonished by her mother for throwing sand in the face of a playmate. "Now you go over there and apologize," the mother demanded.

"No, I won't," the little girl replied. "I'm not sorry I did it. I don't like her."

The mother persisted, louder. The daughter acquiesced. She skulked over to her victim and said, cursorily, that she was sorry, then ran back.

"No, that's not good enough," declared her mother.

"You go back and tell her you're sorry, as if you meant it."

This unfortunately typical scene illustrates the attempt of the culture to impose its values. "Lie," the little girl is told. "Not only lie, but lie in such a way that people do not know you are lying."

Lying comes from our unwillingness to accept ourselves. When I feel dumb or wrong or foolish, I lie so people will not know I am dumb or wrong or foolish. When I am insecure or guilty or ashamed, I lie. When I want to have something I feel I am not supposed to have or something I anticipate someone will prevent me from getting, I lie. When I do not feel capable of dealing with the consequences of the truth, I lie.

The validity of these statements finds support in the current controversy over privacy. Civil rights groups, among others, have made a great deal over the importance of privacy. Surprisingly, I find myself, a long-time, embattled liberal, not agreeing. When I demand privacy, it is because I am ashamed. I even started to write a paper—a psychologist's way of not having to deal personally with a problem—on the right to privacy, until I realized it was bullshit.

Aloneness is wonderful. I love to be alone, often. Privacy, that is, not wanting people to know what I am doing when I am alone, is the cover-up. The more I become comfortable with myself, and the more I accept all the ways I am, the less important is privacy. If I am content with whether I masturbate with both hands, with what I do away from my wife, with what fantasies I have, with how I cheat and steal, or with whatever I do, then I am perfectly content to share them with people. In fact, I prefer that people know, for then I may enter into real human dialogue. I do not have to remain on a superficial, hypocritical level.

The public debate on issues of privacy seems to be off target. Should we know of John Kennedy's sexual exploits? Will it help to reveal the CIA's vagaries? Is it fair to expose Nixon's *Final Days*? Should we know the private lives of our heroes? Should referees use TV replays to help them make decisions?

The wrong aspects of these problems have come into focus. The public issue is stated in terms of whether events should be repressed or ignored: "It's none of our business"; "referees would be embarrassed." When made public, many of these revelations elicit righteousness on the part of public officials: "A President shouldn't do that." "What will our children think?" "I don't want my son to know that Mickey Mantle drank alcohol."

Revealing what is, allows us to grow. We know more about the world than we did prior to the revelation. Suppressing information keeps us from personal expansion and causes social disease just as lies told by an individual are accompanied by physical disease.

The real problem is the hypocrisy of the public reaction, not the revelation itself. The "law-and-order" advocates who violate the law, the "public morality" champions who have mistresses on the public payroll, the "budget cutters" who take long, unnecessary junkets with an entourage of forty, the alcoholics who are appalled at the marijuana users—these behaviors are the source of the problem.

Much gossip is true, as Woodward and Bernstein, Jack Anderson, and muckrakers throughout history have repeatedly shown. Gossip is of such great interest because much of it is true. The great public thirst for the truth is expressed in the outrageous popularity of gossip. However, the public collusion to say what is proper rather than what is true relegates truth to an underground operation and contributes to the low status of gossip. This paradox is exemplified by the *National Enquirer,* a gossip newspaper of the lowest repute—and a circulation of 17 million.

## ALIVENESS

If all social affairs were conducted in honesty, would that diminish sociological ills? Probably.

It certainly would reduce acts of violence. Truth is a substitute for violence.

Suppose I am in a war and I get shot at, I see my buddies die, and I observe cowardice and bravery—spine-tingling events, all. Then I go home and successfully run a gas station for twenty years. What do I talk about when I am having a beer with the boys? I talk about the one time in my life that I felt fully alive, when my emotions were high, my senses keen, and my movements quick. For good or evil, I was using myself.

When war is mentioned, I acknowledge its evil and I voice a wish for world peace, but somewhere in me the urge for excitement puts a brake on my peaceful avowals. My conflict over war is justified by such concepts as "noble" wars, wars that prevent our nation from "getting shoved around," wars for religion, nationhood, or principle. The conflict is expressed on Sunday afternoon when me and Mean Joe Greene sack the quarterback, when I make John Wayne, Clint Eastwood, and Charles Bronson my most popular actors, when I rate movies about murder and destroying life fine (PG), and movies about lovemaking and creating life not fine (X).

Why is my civilian life not more exciting? Because I lie. Because everybody lies. Because talk-show hosts lie when they say that every singer on their program is wonderful and every comedian is hilarious. Because politicians lie when every summit conference is followed by a joint statement written before the conference. Because I lie when I am diplomatic and tactful and I do not "hurt people's feelings." Because I lie to myself when I think what people don't know won't hurt them. Because diplomats tell me what they want me to know, not what is. Because most of my communication is saying what is proper to say, is saying whatever will make people continue liking me, inviting me, patronizing my store, renewing my contract, paying my salary. And all of it has very little to do with how I really feel. After all, I must be practical and realistic.

I have been observing dramas lately to see what effect total honesty would have on them. I am nearing the conclusion that almost all of them would be over in the first act if everyone told the truth. The plot of almost all plays seems to be: "What will happen when everyone finds out the truth?" What will happen when Howard finds out that you have cancer; when Blanche learns that you are in love with her sister; when Charles learns that you are not his real father; when Arthur learns that Guinevere loves Lancelot; when Philip discovers that his barber works for the Russians?

When the truth is told, excitement and aliveness follow. The truth is exciting. Betty Ford caused a national stir by telling the truth about how she would respond to her children's sexual experiences or experiments with marijuana. The public was aghast. The public was also delighted, outraged, excited, and alive. A public figure told the truth. Some people wanted her to run for President in place of her husband.

Telling the truth pops the cork. Out flows the person. Lying blocks self-insight and interpersonal contact. Lying blocks exploration of the self. Every second, the body sends thousands of signals which we shut off because we do not want to hear the truth. As a result, we feel dull and become ill.

Lying blocks me from knowing you. You become another person who says what a person should say, and I am bored. And so are you.

When we do not lie, life becomes exciting—more exciting than violence. People unfold, their depths are plumbed. We connect with each other.

Several years ago, I was on the *Tonight* Show with Johnny Carson, promoting my book *Joy*. I was delighted to be a celebrity and to bring to the masses the word about the marvelous techniques I had collected and created. I had a whole arsenal of new methods, mainly nonverbal.

Carson was intrigued. He gave me thirty minutes on the program, so I had a chance to show how to express anger by pounding on the mattress along with Carson, Ed McMahon, and the guests. Johnny fell backward and I caught him. It was wonderful—everything I had hoped for. Then we had three minutes left and he asked me what else I did in encounter groups.

"We tell the truth," I replied. I felt that the main show was over and now we would just do a short filler and go home.

"How would we do that here?" he asked.

"Well," I said, "it seemed to me that your singer tonight giggled quite a lot and I thought it annoyed you. You winced a few times. If this were a group, I would invite you to tell her directly instead of holding it back and keeping yourself more distant from her."

After a few denials, Carson acknowledged that he did have a slight feeling of that kind once or twice. At my suggestion, he told her directly.

"Oh, I'm so glad you told me," she gushed. "I thought you felt that way and I'm delighted to hear you say it." With that they exchanged warmth and the show ended happily.

The next morning on the streets of New York, I was stopped by at least a dozen people who had seen the show, and, to my astonishment, every one of them commented only about the truth episode. At first I was chagrined. Here I had demonstrated all my wonderful, new methods and apparently no one cared. Their response was to the simple fundamental of encounter—honesty. "Been watching Johnny Carson for four years, and that's the first time I've seen him real," was the tenor of their comments. They felt they had gotten to know their long-time acquaintance simply because he was honest.

It was then that I began to see the excitement of

honesty. The nonverbal techniques were fine, but the
thrill of seeing someone tell the truth overwhelmed all
else. With truth comes excitement in living, hence the
need for violence in order to feel alive is greatly
lessened. You hold great excitement for me when I
know what you are like, how you feel, what you think,
what you worry about, what makes you happy. The
personal underworld is the great quest, the great adventure. Lying masks it and muffles our lives so that,
like a dying phonograph record, we slowly wind down
to lifelessness.

## AWARENESS

Increased self-awareness begins with a commitment
to look inside. Accepting the principle of choice
means that the power to know myself lies within me.
I will know myself best when I experience situations
that call upon my full capacity.

I will also know myself best when I overcome the
fear of looking at what I truly am. I must sacrifice
evaluation for discovery, no matter what I may discover, no matter how much energy I have put into
hiding parts of me from myself. I must become more
acquainted with my body.

Some techniques for increasing self-awareness are
guru-oriented and some are self-oriented. Guru-oriented approaches claim that if you follow the guru you
will find enlightenment. Self-oriented approaches
create conditions that are designed to lead you to find
your own strength.

One basic difference between the self-oriented
approaches, such as the Feldenkrais technique, fasting,
encounter, and imagery, and the guru-oriented approaches, such as yoga, rolfing, Western medicine, and
behavior modification, is this: Self-oriented approaches
rely on the bodymind to know what is best for it.
They concentrate on presenting options and on in-

creasing awareness of the differences between options. Guru-oriented approaches train the bodymind in the correct way, as decided by an outside authority.

The difference between the two approaches is well illustrated by the physical aspects of the Arica training and the Feldenkrais exercises. When Arica teaches an exercise that requires standing with the feet apart, the instructor specifies the distance between the feet as equal to the length of the lower arm. If I assume a different stance, the instructor corrects me. I am correct when I have remembered and carried out the instructions properly. The instructions ultimately come from the Arica guru, Oscar Ichazo.

When a Feldenkrais exercise requires feet apart, I am instructed to put my feet very close together and to focus my awareness on the comfort I feel. Then I am to place my legs wide apart and to be aware of how pleasurable that position is. Then I am to keep shifting the distance between those points until I feel most comfortable. The comfortable position is "correct." I know what is right through reference to myself and to my own feelings.

Guru-oriented techniques work especially well for people who are in a very confused state and who want to become more disciplined. I have seen many people bring their lives into much better order by following a guru. Some remain as followers and some eventually leave, having received as much as they feel they want. If people remain followers too long, I suspect that the guru is creating conditions in which people find it easy to be followers.

The best gurus have no followers—or, at least do not have them for very long.

To be consistent with the principles of finding the joyful life, a teacher of a self-oriented method creates conditions within which people choose to grow. Techniques that follow the natural—encounter, imagery, fasting, and Feldenkrais—are self-oriented methods.

Feldenkrais is very clear on this point in his exercises.[46] His instructions are: to experience all movements or positions and to become aware of how they feel in the body. He assumes the body will naturally select the movement that is most efficient in terms of energy, strength, stamina, and flexibility.

In fasting, the bodymind is assumed to know how, and to be best equipped, to heal itself and to select the food that is more nutritious and life-giving. The fast is a way to increase body awareness by purification and removal of excess fatty tissue.

In guided imagery, the bodymind is assumed to travel, in fantasy, to those areas of the body in which problems exist and, through the mechanism of daydream, aided by a guide, to eliminate that problem. One job of the guide is to allow and to encourage the fantasizer to explore all the possibilities in the daydream. If there are any aspects that are frightening, the fantasizer continues until those aspects are mastered and the fear is gone. All options are available, all have been explored, and all may be utilized.

As a member of an encounter group, you are encouraged to experience all your options and to observe how you feel. At the same time, you are encouraged to learn to read your body signals so that you better may know the truth. Instead of being told, for example, that you should stay married, you are encouraged to say: "I want to stay married," then to say: "I do not want to stay married," and to observe how you feel when you say each. Your feeling will tell you which you really want to do.

The bodymind chooses. It is the pivot. The self-oriented methods assume that the pivot is the source of ultimate knowledge, the God within.

To work, all self-oriented methods require that the bodymind be aware of all options, of how each option feels, and of how each differs from the others. It requires that the bodymind be free to experience each option without fear. Then the bodymind will choose the true option—the one that is most in accord with its own being.

To help people explore their own potential, these

techniques focus on revealing and exploring options. If you fear the consequences of one option, it is often valuable to experience it. Feldenkrais teaches you to stand on your head by teaching you how not to stand on your head. First you learn how to fall over; then you learn how to be off-balance. Feel it, experience it, be aware of it. Then balance so that you do not feel any of these things. And there you are, standing on your head!

"Do all the catastrophes first," he says. The fears in your body prevent you from standing on your head. Experience the fears first; do them gradually and easily. Then do them over and over until they are no longer fears.

Sharon was about to visit her family for the holidays. Her fear of her father had always been very great. At the prospect of seeing him with her child, she became ill. In an encounter group, she spoke to a pillow representing her father. She told him her fears. She told him all the things she had never said. She played his role. She cried, she pleaded, she hugged him. When it was over, she had lived through all of her anticipated catastrophes.

Then Sharon went home and confronted her father. The result was astonishing. It was easy. He responded far better than she had imagined. She was very strong, and they wound up loving at a depth they had not reached before.

Experiencing the catastrophes before the actual event is the key to overcoming fears. Do them, defang them, do them gradually, do them at your own pace. Do them repeatedly, exhaustively, until there is no more fear. Then act. You will have experienced the options that are preventing you from proceeding and, through this method, eliminated them yourself.

Eyesight provides another example of exploring options. From my youth, I was encouraged to see "correctly." Correctly meant that I should see everything in sharp focus. Of all the possible positions in which I can focus my eyes, only one of these positions is considered desirable. If I do not see "properly," I am urged to acquire artificial aids, glasses or contacts, to focus sharply.

In fact, my eyes are capable of many degrees of "out-of-focus" seeing. I see the world very differently when my eyes are out of focus. I see a larger perspective and not so much detail. I see auras around people and objects, providing I defocus my eyes. Mystically inclined people feel they see a different level of reality when not focusing.

If I followed the notion of options, I would develop my ability to focus my eyes along the whole continuum of possibilities, and I would explore the characteristics of each point of focus. Reading requires sharp focus. Driving may be done best with a relaxed focus so that relative motion is sensed readily. Enjoyment of sunsets may be greater with considerable defocusing.

L. L. Thurstone, the renowned psychologist, once had an idea for a substitute for the Rorschach projective test. Instead of asking people to report what they saw in a historically chosen set of inkblots, Thurstone would have them look at one picture very much out of focus and report what they saw. Then, in ten equal stages, he would gradually focus the picture, asking for a description after each readjustment of the picture. This ingenious technique could also be used to train people to learn focus options and to observe the different perceptions available.

The implication for teaching is this: Do not teach the bodymind to learn to accomplish a specific task. Teach it to find out how each point of the range may be used best, then how each combination may be used best.

## HEALTH AND ILLNESS

With awareness comes control of the body. Illness and injury may be avoided. If I am aware of a part of my body, I can control it. I am able to put it into any state I wish. In biofeedback, awareness of single muscles has been achieved so that a person can contract or relax that muscle at will. Heart rate may be varied, digestion hastened, and pain reduced through awareness.

Athletes are injured in those areas from which they have withdrawn awareness. If I injure my shoulder, I tend to take my attention out of that shoulder. It hurts and I do not want to experience the hurt. If I am told that moving my pelvis or rolling my eyes is naughty, I withdraw my awareness from those areas; I dissociate myself from them. If my hand was slapped frequently for misdeeds, I act as if it is not my hand, and I have difficulty feeling it. If my entire body is criticized as evil, lustful, and violent, I may withdraw my senses from it and numb myself below the neck.

When I do these things, I am at war with myself. My attitude toward the rejected parts is either to want to punish them or to let them take care of themselves without my assistance. My body can eat what it wants, exercise itself, do anything while I am not involved. My hand needs punishment so I will "accidentally" hit it with a hammer, slam a door on it, bend a finger playing ball, or smash it into a wall. I do not let myself know what these parts are sensing, whether they feel comfortable or painful, relaxed or tense, hot or cold, healthy or diseased.

As a result, when potentially toxic materials enter these alienated parts, I do not choose to oppose them, and my body parts become ill. Or I do not choose to resist a potentially injury-producing situation. The parts of my body that become ill or injured are the parts from which I have withdrawn awareness or, to put it another way, that I have with awareness chosen to make ill or injured.

A radiologist friend reported that his profession has a well-kept secret. Many tumors removed from patients look like little people. In an eerie way, it is as though the patient's empty rooms, those which are not occupied by awareness, have been moved in on by new tenants.

Any muscle tension, irritation, inflammation, or other illness is the result of a conflict of which I am not allowing myself to be aware. If I choose not to be aware of the conflict, then my body is obliged to "embody" the conflict. If I allow myself total self-awareness, I may choose not to be ill.

All illness is psychosomatic in the sense that I choose my illness in response to my present life situation. Much has been learned through the psychosomatic investigations of the last half century. I shall here present a simple paradigm for understanding the principles underlying the psychosomatic function, along with a few examples.

Not only is illness the result of out-of-awareness conflict, but the particular illness I choose follows logically from my life-style. The key to understanding the specificity of illness lies in children's books on the body. Each part of the body is described in colloquial terms as if the body were a community in which each organ and system has a specific function. Circulation is the transportation system, communication is handled by the nervous system, excretion is the garbage disposal system, and so on. Taking this description literally, and assuming that there is a parallel between the person's intrapsychic, interpersonal, and physiological lives, provides the key to understanding selection of ailments.

To explore the meaning of the illness in their lives, I have been talking to several people who have had hepatitis. Hepatitis is an inflammation of the liver. The liver is an organ of assimilation. It processes and stores nutrients and waste products (urea). In other words, its job is to use the substances that are nourishing to the body and to help eliminate those which are not usable or which are potentially harmful. Taking this function literally, I assume that if I have hepatitis, I am having difficulty in my life using the things that are good for me and getting rid of those which are toxic, and that I am not aware of having that difficulty. Since I am not dealing with the conflict with my awareness, my body must deal with it.

The hepatitis patients I have spoken to have all reported being in some kind of transition at the time of contracting the disease. Some were moving, some were changing jobs, some were in the midst of divorce. The issues of whether they were making the right decision and of how to adapt to their new situations were central in their lives and, they reported, not being given much thought. Difficulty with choosing those parts of their lives which were productive and in eliminating those which were poisonous parallel a problem with the function of the liver.

Leukemia means that the body produces too many white blood cells, the defenders against disease, and too few red blood cells, the carriers of body nutrients. The leukemia patient is literally too defensive. Leukemia patients often have a feeling of vulnerability and defenselessness. Apparently, the production of excessive defenses in the body is an attempt to compensate for the feeling of having too few defenses.

On a larger scale, there is national leukemia. Sixty percent of the national budget of the United States goes for defense (white cells), with the result that many of our internal activities (red cells), like employment and housing, are undernourished, that is, not provided with enough funding.

One of the most consistent findings in psychosomatic literature is that hyperthyroid people tend to be dependent. The thyroid hormone, thyroxin, controls metabolic rate, growth, and maturation. If I feel dependent and want to be more mature, and I am not aware of this conflict, I may compensate for my feeling by producing an excess of the maturation hormone, just as the leukemia patient compensates for a feeling of defenselessness by producing an excess of defenders.

These are just a few examples. The psychosomatic literature is extensive, and several diseases have been described in similar terms.[47] I am suggesting here that there is a simple way to understand illness.

Illness arises from an out-of-awareness conflict. It is expressed by the part of the body that corresponds, literally, to the conflict. The illness may either express the conflict, as in hepatitis, or it may compensate for inadequate feelings, as in leukemia and hyperthyroidism. In the section on Basic Dimensions below (page 125) a more precise framework is presented for understanding the selection of specific illnesses.

Illness is part of the life-style. I have observed many cases where severe illness caused little life change. Being a very cautious woman, Rachel never exerted herself physically but used her clever, acerbic wit to mock exercise. She planned well in advance for every activity and was considerably upset when plans changed. She cautioned her children to get plenty of sleep and to minimize risks. She stage-managed what she considered her major events, like telling her children about adult illness, with great gravity on the assumption that the children were very fragile and could only cope if given great support. Her life was primarily sedentary and domestic. She suffered quietly. ("Oh, don't bother about me.")

Then Rachel developed cancer of the lymph system. She was operated on and had her spleen removed. Upon recovery, her life-style was marked by caution, lack of risk-taking, and very careful planning because she had cancer. In other words, her previous life-style barely changed. She had been living as if she had cancer, and when she developed it, nothing changed. Her life-style had prepared her to live like a cancer patient.

# COMPLETION

> To think and to will without action, when one
> is able to act, is like a flame shut up in a
> vessel, which dies away; or like a seed cast
> upon sand, which does not grow up, but per-
> ishes with its power of germination . . .
> —Emanuel Swedenborg

How do I prevent my bodymind from unfolding
naturally? How are the principles of truth and choice
carried into my life? What are the consequences of a
lack of awareness, honesty, and self-responsibility?

The Principle of Completion describes the mechanisms of maturation and the development of bodymind
problems.

## ENERGY CYCLES

Human behavior may be perceived as a series of
energy cycles. A cycle begins with some type of imbalance—discomfort, desire, anxiety, wonder—something that serves to *motivate* me to change my state
so as to satisfy the imbalance either by reducing the
discomfort or anxiety or by satisfying the desire or
wonder. I then mobilize my resources to reduce the
imbalance. I *prepare* myself to do something by thinking, planning, and preparing my body for some kind
of movement. Discharge comes next, expressing in
*action* the behavior for which I have prepared. Action
leads to a rebalance, or *feeling*, determined by how

close the action came to satisfying the motivating imbalance.

In terms of the functions of the nervous system, this cycle is: sensing, thinking, moving, feeling. Other authors have presented similar schema from the perspectives of sociology, physiology, and scientific method.[48]

Completion of energy cycles results in learning and maturation. I am constantly living through these cycles. This constitutes experience.

Difficulties arise when energy cycles are not completed. Blockages occur at each point in the cycle and affect all levels of being: interpersonal, intrapsychic, physical. I may block each phase in the energy cycle by 1) denying it, or 2) by letting it happen and then distorting it.

## MOTIVATION

The energy cycle begins with whatever impinges upon my nervous system from outside or inside my skin—I itch, I want sex, I am bored, I want to learn, I feel depressed. I experience the imbalance. If it is pleasing, I simply continue to experience it. If I perceive that the imbalance would be more pleasant if it were balanced, I may proceed to change my state.

I block myself from completing the energy cycle by denial or by distortion of the experience being motivated.

*Denying* the imbalance is accomplished through a process of self-deception. I choose not to acknowledge that I feel unbalanced. I repress the sensation. I blunt my senses so that I do not see things clearly, or hear, or smell, or feel with discrimination. I dull my senses and deny that there is any imbalance, any problem in my life. "Everything is fine." I can even become condescending about my condition. "I don't understand why people need psychotherapy. I have no problems. If I did, I would just take a walk and feel fine."

*Distortion* involves not seeing clearly what is happening. "I don't feel good, but I'm sure it's just something I ate." Sometimes I acknowledge the imbalance and choose not to identify it. "Something doesn't feel right, but I don't know what it is."

If blockage at this stage becomes my typical behavior, my body is dull, out of touch, prone to illness and injury since I have no awareness of my body sensations.

### Motivation Block

| | |
|---|---|
| Psychological: | I am unaware. |
| Nervous System: | I will not sense. |
| Body: | Neglected. |

### PREPARATION

If I allow the energy cycle to continue, after identifying the imbalance, I prepare to take action to bring about a rebalance. I think of what to do and my brain sends a pattern of impulses to my muscles to prepare for a certain sequence of movements.

*Denying* the preparation phase takes the form of not letting myself and/or others know that I am planning something. "Who, me? I would certainly never think of doing a thing like that. What kind of person do you think I am?" Sometimes someone will point out that my fist is clenched while I am denying being angry toward someone. I have denied my preparation.

*Distortion* of preparation is nicely illustrated by W. C. Fields movies when he raises his hand to hit a child, spots his wife, and acts as if he is adjusting his hat. Sometimes I distort my intention from myself by believing, for example, that I am really planning to withhold a secret from you "for your own good," when I am really doing it to get revenge.

My body never prepares itself for movement. Muscles do not get exercised and have no tone.

Both denial and distortion stop the energy cycle before Preparation is complete.

### Preparation Block

| Psychological: | I am undecided. |
| Nervous System: | I will not think. |
| Body: | Toneless. |

#### ACTION

If I allow myself to be aware of my imbalance and I prepare to act, the next stage is to take action, to discharge the energy I have mobilized. I do something, I use my muscular system, including my vocal cords, to move until I reach a new balance.

*Denying* action includes statements such as: "I didn't say that"; "I certainly didn't do a thing like that." With the introduction of tape recordings, people are often amazed to find that they did say or do something they have blocked completely. I may deliberately deny something I know I have done, or I may deceive myself into feeling I did not do it. One of the best-known acts of denial of action is the famous statement: "I am not a crook."

*Distortion* of action takes the form of reinterpreting or undoing a previous action. I recently made a deal with someone to produce a workshop for me. He would produce it, I would do it, and we would divide the money fifty-fifty. As the time approached, I began to think I had made a bad deal and that I should get a higher percentage. I decided to call him to make certain he understood that expenses came out of his fifty percent. A friend to whom I told this intention questioned what I was up to. After giving a detailed, logical, and irritated justification for my position, I calmed down and got in touch with what was really happening.

I had made a deal I regretted. I felt like a patsy, like I had been stupid for entering into the deal. By distorting what had happened, through an excruciatingly legal argument, I was attempting to undo my stupidity by acting as though the agreement had never been made. In fact, my action was legally defensible because we had never explicitly assigned expenses. However, I knew that when we entered into the agreement I assumed we would share the expenses. That was the usual arrangement, and I was trying to deny it. I never made that phone call.

If I am characteristically conflicted over action, the energy in my body does not get discharged. I feel irritable and impatient. I block my body just before I take action. Since most movement is done with the arms and legs, I develop tension in the upper arms and shoulders and in the upper legs.

### Action Block

| Psychological: | I am stuck. |
| --- | --- |
| Nervous System: | I will not move. |
| Body: | Blocked. |

### FEELING

Successful completion of an energy cycle includes motivation, preparation, action, and the full experience of the feeling that follows the completed action. If the act is successful, the new balance in the body-mind will feel satisfactory and will require no further attention. If not, a new energy cycle begins with a new plan of preparation, usually with a better chance of success because it may use the experience of the last energy cycle.

*Denying* the feeling cuts off full experiencing. If I have difficulty with affection, I may ignore or make a joke when someone compliments me. Sometimes when I am complimented after a lecture, I very soberly thank the person. I have to remind myself that it is all right to smile. I realize that I am attempting mightily not to express or even to feel the pleasure. Inside me, however, there is a little boy jumping up and down, clapping his hands, and saying: "Whee! Say more."

I may deny feeling the success of an action or I

may deny feeling the failure of an action. Many years
ago, I was trying to find out (motivation) why breaking
up with my college sweetheart made me feel so miserable. As I probed further with friends, I discovered that
the reason for my depression was that I was afraid my
friends would think less of me (preparation). I
checked it out with them (action) and found they did
not think less of me. I felt content. However, the next
morning I awoke feeling miserable and realized I had
been denying my true feeling, which was not content-
ment at all, but, rather, no change (feeling).

*Distortion* of feeling also causes difficulties. Don was
a twenty-one-year-old man who loved his father and
felt his father respected him a great deal and, yes,
loved him too. As we explored this relationship, it
turned out that he only saw his father twice a month
("Which is okay."), that he does not confide in his
father ("I have other friends for that."), that his
father did not really care to hear about his personal
matters ("But he doesn't condemn me."), and that if
he were a father, Don would like to hear personal
matters from his son ("Yes, yes, I really would.").

What started out as a description of a "minor issue"
was revealed as a major one as Don allowed himself
to experience his true feeling about the relationship.
He had apparently cut off feeling for all people, denying that he had any major problems in order not to
experience his disappointment and sadness at not feeling more loved. If he allowed himself to feel fully,
he would have to face that sadness. As a result, Don
went through life without major upset but, in a quiet-
voiced, low-key way, feeling very little. It was the lack
of feeling and aliveness that bothered him and provided
his motivation to explore and to discover the price he
was paying for his unawareness.

In the body, refusal to experience the feelings fully
leads to muscles remaining tight and rigid. Good feeling
requires relaxation of the muscles.

The flexors, the muscles that close the angles of
the joints, are used for accomplishment and for defense.

They close up the body. The extensors, the muscles that open the joints, are the happy muscles. When a football player is running down the field for a touchdown, he is generally hunched over, using his flexors to achieve his purpose. After he crosses the goal line, he exults by throwing his arms in the air, using his extensors to express his joy.

People who do not let themselves relax and enjoy their achievements tend to have rigid bodies and an empty feeling following accomplishment. Suicides of "successful" people often result from this blockage.

### Feeling Block

| Psychological: | I am non-feeling. |
| Nervous System: | I will not feel. |
| Body: | Armored. |

## BODYMIND PROBLEMS

There are two types of emotional problems, denials (unfinished experience) and distortions (lies). Both result from blocked or incomplete energy cycles. Suppressed experience never dies. It does not even fade away. It just gets pushed back into the body and is held there by a physical aberration, usually a muscle tension.

Mary's life had been dormant for many years, and her sexual attitudes and feelings toward children were filled with fear and guilt. I asked her to shut her eyes and let a picture come into her head.[13] Immediately, she saw a picture of an event for which she had denied all feeling, an abortion she had twenty years earlier. The abortion energy cycle had been blocked between the action and feeling phases. In the fantasy, she relived the experience, but this time she allowed herself to feel the terror, fear, shame, guilt, excitement, and other feelings that she had successfully suppressed. She cried, screamed, sobbed, and whimpered. When it was over she felt refreshed and greatly relieved. She was now capable of dealing with sexuality and children in a more realistic way. The abortion energy cycle was completed and was no longer stuck in her.

Mine was the sixth group Lil had attended with the express intent of dealing with her dead father. She had become a very skilled encounter bum. She knew how to work on straightening out her relation with her father. "If only my mother had allowed me to go to his funeral. I was only five. I didn't understand." She would talk to her father, beat on a pillow representing him, embrace him, plead with him, cry to him, all in the best psychodramatic, gestalt, and bioenergetic styles. Then she would feel fine . . . for a few moments.

I asked her to consider the possibility that her failure to resolve the issue of her father after repeated attempts was due to a lie. She assented. "Please consider the possibility that you didn't want to go to the funeral. It was your choice, not your mother's." Lil looked up with that telltale sign of someone whose game has been exposed. Although she was not aware of her game, she was aware that it was a game after it was pointed out. She recalled that she had arranged the situation so that her mother would not let her go to the funeral. She really had not wanted to go. With that realization Lil heaved a sigh of relief, grabbed the pillow representing her father, and said to it," So long, it's been good to know you," gave it a hug, put it aside, and rejoined the group. The distortion of the action phase had been corrected and she could complete the cycle. The issue was never mentioned again.

These problems are like the difficulties in a crossword puzzle.

Mary's problem was that, by her denial, she had not fully experienced her feelings at the time of the abortion. This is equivalent to not knowing a definition in a crossword puzzle. It is an incomplete experience. Because she did not want to deal with the abortion, her sexual life remained neglected.

Lil's difficulty was equivalent to putting a wrong

word into the puzzle. Her lie required distorting and
giving old interpretations to subsequent events to make
them consistent with the lie, just as putting a wrong
word into a puzzle requires weird convolutions of many
other words.

Nations, too, have emotional illness when lies exist
in their history. Concurrent and subsequent events must
be given distorted interpretations in order to rationalize
the lie. The effect on the country of the revelations
of Wategate, the CIA, and the FBI is a superb
example of a nation getting emotionally better by
correcting lies. The puzzling nature of oddly contra-
dictory governmental statements, inexplicable attitudes
of nations like Chile, and the extreme "paranoid"
behavior of the revolutionaries of the 1960s may better
be understood as the truth is revealed.

I suspect that the undiminished interest in the
assassination of John F. Kennedy is due to the fact
that the official interpretation of the event (Warren
Commission) is a lie. That so many misunderstandings
surrounding the event defy logic keeps the issue alive
just as Lil's father remained alive for her. Our understanding of history, of ballistics, of coincidence, of con-
spiracy, of power, and of presidents does not make a
great deal of sense if we accept the Warren Commission
findings, so we squirm about, trying to find the explanation that will relieve us of our uneasy feelings and
restore logic to this wide variety of unexplained events.


## COMPLETING CYCLES

Often, I behave in certain ways that mystify me.
Why do I become ill? Why do I ruin relationships
just when they are becoming close? Why do I get
jealous when it pains me so? It is hard for me to
understand why I choose to act in ways that are painful
and ineffective. Energy cycles help clarify this mystery.

In these cases, I am choosing a course of action and
not letting myself know about it. I choose it because

I am trying to complete an energy cycle I never finished. Tension from the imbalance continues to impel me to action. In psychoanalysis, the concept of transference describes a similar phenomenon. I treat my wife badly because I am trying to resolve my unfinished business with my mother.

Martina was timid and withdrawn and did not want to be. Her left shoulder was held very high, while her lower arms were thin and pale and appeared to lack energy. She did not want her shoulder and arms in this condition and could not understand why she chose them to be this way. After a rolfing and a fantasy,[49] the unfinished energy cycle that accounted for her behavior and for her body began to emerge. Following is Martina's account of her experience.

At the beginning of the week (in the workshop) . . . Henry told me to fuck off. I felt totally rejected by everybody, miserable. I withdrew from the group and was playing poor little me, come and get me. Nobody came, and I kept feeling rejected. Frank and Tom said they didn't like me and it hurt. I felt that Don was losing interest in me, so I was hurting.

Yesterday afternoon, I was walking around feeling my pain. I was feeling like a woman about to give birth to a child, so when the group met, it didn't take much for me to start crying. We were standing in the nude, having our bodies analyzed. Will got very interested in my shoulders and in my expression of fear. So Don did some rolfing in my shoulders. As soon as he touched a point in my left shoulder, I felt a very painful pull. Then Will took me into a guided fantasy. He asked me to become little and to go to my shoulders and see what was there. Nothing was happening. I was aware of the noise in the room, and I was aware of the people and thinking that I wasn't going to get anywhere and everybody was going to get angry and reject me more. Then Will asked me if I was seeing any colors. I was seeing a light purple. Then I lost awareness of sounds and people and felt that someone was pulling me. I was three or four years old and she had terrible anger and hate expressed on her face. Will asked me to see what I did to make her so angry. I saw my father holding me. I was a baby. It felt very good to be loved by him. He was in the first house we lived in when I was little, and he looked very young and handsome.

Then my mother came into the picture. He was kind of indifferent toward her, and very connected with me, and she was jealous and was pulling me away. I felt she hated me, she rejected me, she didn't want me to be born. She wanted me to disappear. My father wasn't there, and I cried and cried and felt the pain fully until I felt I was back in the room. I felt very good.

After this experience, Martina's shoulder was noticeably lower, almost even with her right shoulder. Apparently, raising her shoulder and withdrawing energy from her arms was a way of attempting to avoid pain and to pull free of her angry mother. Her timidity and reliance on being a cute little girl also enabled her to avoid angering her mother. Never having resolved this situation—never having completed this energy cycle—Martina continued to cope with it both physically and behaviorally. Becoming aware of and reliving the situation to a more successful conclusion resulted in a withdrawal of the need to hang on to the situation. Martina could now stop her unwanted behavior.

If I want to be truly facilitating to you, a person with an incomplete energy cycle, I use the homeopathic principle,[50] and create conditions that encourage you to complete the cycle. If you are crying, it is usually not helpful to "comfort" you by urging you to stop crying. Stopping the crying is blocking the energy cycle in the action phase; you are left with an incomplete act. You must find some other place and time to finish crying. Similarly, holding back someone who is violent, without allowing (acceptable) discharge of the angry energy, leaves the act incomplete. It is more helpful to allow the energy cycle to be completed in an acceptable way and then to examine what happened.

If your actions are harmful, I assume you are acting on an out-of-awareness level. If I wish to be helpful, I create conditions under which you may choose to become more aware. If, for example, you are angry at a critic, you may come to realize that you are choosing to be angry. You are not allowing yourself to be aware that your anger is a cover-up for feeling hurt, and that you are feeling angry because you really feel your accuser is right.

All these awarenesses allow you to deal more effectively with the situation. External suppression prevents this evolution and would have to be administered constantly. The only constructive function of outside suppression is to delay the execution of an act you would not want to have performed had you allowed yourself more awareness. Murder or suicide are examples of this.

When you are unaware, incomplete energy cycles are brought to your awareness and resolved through some re-experiencing technique—psychoanalysis, psychodrama, gestalt, primal, rebirthing fantasy—they no longer direct your behavior. You then have the choice to make a decision with awareness. If all your unaware energy cycles are brought to awareness and completed, then all of your choices are made with awareness, with your will.

When two or more people enter into an interaction, they select the experience that will allow them to complete energy cycles, or they will create new ones they can complete together. This is one explanation of love relations. We spend a few years working out many of the cycles that we can use each other to complete. Then together we create new ones that are here-and-now cycles, more free of old encumbrances. "Old friends" are those with whom you have already completed most of your old cycles.

Each person allows me to work out certain cycles with them. Some male figures make it easier for me to complete my unfinished father feelings. In that sense, I use them. And that is fine. They use me too.

In any close relation, people use each other. I use you to help me attain my next level of evolution. Perhaps you have the spontaneity I lack, so I use you to initiate a conversation into which I can then follow you. And you use my stability to keep you from doing foolish things. It is important that we use each other if our relationship is to be mutually profitable.

Energy cycles are to be experienced fully and not blocked. Our objective is the free flow of energy through all phases of the cycle.

# BASIC DIMENSIONS

I hate quotations. Tell me what you know.
—Ralph Waldo Emerson

The principle of basic dimensions is probably more unique to the present author than are any of the other principles. It was first presented in 1958 and has been elaborated in several succeeding books.[51] The Principle of Basic Dimensions allows for a more detailed elaboration of the holistic approach.

Investigations of social organization lead to the discovery of three fundamental dimensions that describe the important phenomena. Whether these investigations begin with group behavior, personality types, parent-child relations, patterns of delinquency, or, as shall be described below, organ systems of the body, the same dimensions emerge.

In order to function effectively, organisms must establish and maintain certain balances between the inside and the outside of their boundaries. These balances apply to the physical world and to the social world. For example, humans seek enough water inside their skins to avoid thirst, and little enough to avoid drowning. Similarly, organisms desire a certain amount of distance and a certain amount of closeness with other people. Imbalances in these physical and social arenas are the motivators that originate energy cycles.

The basic dimensions of social imbalances arise from two sources: the interaction of the infant with other human beings as it develops into an adult, and the necessary requirements of group action.

## INDIVIDUAL DEVELOPMENT

When an infant is born, for its own survival, it must make contact with other humans. It is well established that lack of human contact for a very young infant leads to retardation, illness, and death.[52] The desire for contact or inclusion in the human family is the interpersonal parallel to the oral stage described by the psychoanalysts. The analysts focus on the primary erogenous zone, the mouth, where there is the greatest stimulation and need. *Inclusion* is the dominant human relationship occurring during the first stages of life.

Following the period of inclusion, the infant enters an era of socialization in which the primary human relation centers around distribution of power and responsibility. Then follows a resolution of how much the child runs its own life and how much it follows the orders of its parents and other adults. The psychoanalyst describes this period, ages two to four years, as the anal stage, focusing on the power struggle that takes place around toilet training. In this struggle, the child experiences its first real bargaining power, withholding feces. The interpersonal aspect of this stage concerns the resolution of *control* of the child's life.

As the child matures, the complexity of love and affectional relations emerges as the central interpersonal event. Love, sacrifice, jealousy of mother's relation with father, sibling rivalry, friendships with playmates, all present themselves to the child at ages four to six years. Again focusing on the erogenous zone, the psychoanalysts call this the phallic or genital stage, where the family romance, the oedipal situation, occurs. The classical rivalry of the son with the father for the mother's love highlights the primary interpersonal concern, *affection*.

Inclusion, control, and affection are the interpersonal aspects of the oral, anal, and phallic stages.

## GROUP FORMATION

For a group to exist, it must define itself as a group. Boundaries must be established such that it is clear who is in and who is out of the group. In ancient and some modern tribes, initiation rites, rites of passage, established tribal membership. In modern groups, there are similar ceremonies—voting, paying dues, passing tests, having a certain lineage, being born of particular parents, promising to uphold certain principles. Whatever the technique, the group is formed through a specific procedure defining *inclusion* into the group.

Once formed, the group differentiates roles and distributes power. Tribes often established a leader through tests of strength or through age. Families determine relations to each other through sex-roles or through abilities. New organizations create bylaws and elect officers. However it is done, the group allocates tasks and establishes the power relations among members. These procedures establish patterns of *control*.

No matter how efficient the group, if it is to survive, personal ties must be established among group members. If no attention is paid to feelings among people, rivalries build, personal desires are not met, people sabotage or leave the group, and group life is over. *Affectional* bonds through family, social affairs, sharing, or personal benefits become established for the group to survive.

In the formation of groups, there emerge the same dimensions that arose in child development, namely, inclusion, control, and affection. These three areas appear at all levels of social organization. Understanding them simplifies understanding the source of the imbalances and motivations of people, groups, nations, and even body parts.

## INCLUSION

Inclusion behavior refers to association between people—exclusion, inclusion, belonging, togetherness. The desire to be included manifests itself as wanting attention, wanting interaction, and being uniquely distinguishable from other people. To be fully identifiable implies that someone is interested enough in me to discover my unique characteristics.

The issue of commitment arises at the outset of group relations. In the initial testing of a relationship, I usually present myself to others to discover what facet of myself will interest them. If I am not sure that others care about what I have to say, I may be silent.

Inclusion does not involve strong emotional attachments to individuals, as does affection. My inclusion preoccupation is with prominence rather than with dominance, as it is in control. Since inclusion involves the process of group formation, it usually occurs as the earliest interpersonal issue in the life of a group. I first decide whether I want to be part of the group, whether I want to be in or out.

Underlying my behavior in all three areas is my self-concept, how I really feel about myself. My self-concept is usually partly conscious and partly unconscious.

In the area of inclusion, my behavior is determined by how I feel about my *significance* as a person. If I have low self-esteem with regard to being significant, my inclusion behavior tends to be extreme and anxious. Either I try hard to have people pay attention to me, the oversocial, or I will withdraw from people, the undersocial.

When I am *undersocial*, I am introverted and withdrawn. I want to maintain distance between myself and others and I do not want to get enmeshed with others and, thereby, to lose my privacy. Unconsciously,

I definitely want others to pay attention to me. My greatest fear is that people will ignore me and will leave me behind. My unaware attitude is: "Since no one is interested in me, I am not going to risk being ignored. I will stay away from people and get along by myself." I use self-sufficiency as a technique for existing without other people. Behind my withdrawal is the private feeling that other people do not understand me. Unawarely, I feel that, since no one ever considered me important enough to give me attention, I must be of no value whatsoever. My deepest anxiety is that I am worthless, insignificant, and unimportant.

When I am *oversocial,* I am extroverted. I seek people incessantly and I want them to seek me out. I fear they will ignore me. My unaware feelings are the same as those of the undersocial, but my overt behavior is the opposite. My unaware attitude is: "Although I know no one is interested in me, I will make people pay attention to me in any way I can." I always seek companionship, for I cannot stand to be alone. My interpersonal behavior is designed to focus attention on myself, to make other people notice me, and to be prominent. My direct method is to be an intense, exhibitionistic participant. By forcing myself on the group, I force the group to focus their attention on me. My subtle technique for gaining attention is to seek to be powerful (control) or to be well-liked (affection). My inclusion problems often lead me to vacillate between oversocial and undersocial behavior.

When I am *social,* one whose problem of inclusion was successfully resolved in childhood, my interaction with people presents no problem. I am comfortable with or without others. I can be a high or low participant in a group, without feeling anxious. I am capable of strong commitment to and involvement with certain groups, and I can also withhold commitment if I feel it is appropriate to do so. I feel that I am a worthwhile, significant person.

The inclusion problem is *in or out.* Inclusion interaction centers on *encounter*. The inclusion anxiety is that I am *insignificant*.

## CONTROL

Control behavior refers to the decision-making process between people in the areas of power, influence, and authority. The desire for control varies along a continuum, from my desire for authority over others (and therefore over my future) to my wish to be controlled and to have responsibility lifted from me.

In an argument, if I am seeking inclusion, or prominence, I want to be one of the participants in the argument. If I am seeking control, I want to be a winner or to be on the same side as the winner. If forced to choose, the prominence-seeker prefers to be a losing participant, while the dominance-seeker prefers to be a winning nonparticipant.

Control behavior is manifested also toward people who try to control. Expression of independence and rebellion exemplify a lack of willingness to be controlled, while compliance, submission, and taking orders indicate various degrees of accepting control.

There is no necessary relation between my behavior toward controlling others and my behavior toward being controlled. Sergeants may dominate their subordinates and accept orders from their lieutenants with pleasure and gratitude, while neighborhood bullies may dominate their peers but not rebel against their parents.

Control behavior differs from inclusion behavior in that it does not require prominence. The "power behind the throne" is a role that simultaneously fulfills a high control desire and a low wish for inclusion, while the "comedian" may be a high-inclusion person with a low desire for control.

Control problems follow those of inclusion in the development of a group and in interpersonal relationships. Once a group has formed, it begins to differentiate. Different people take or seek different roles, and power struggles, competition, and influence become central issues. The typical interaction around these issues is confrontation.

Underlying my behavior in the control area is my feeling of *competence*. If I feel unable to cope with the world, inadequate, or incapable of keeping up with other people, then my control behavior is extreme and anxious. I withdraw from positions of power and responsibility, the abdicrat, or I try to dominate others, the autocrat.

When I am an *abdicrat*, I abdicate my power. I take a subordinate position where I will not have to take responsibility for making decisions. I want other people to relieve me of my obligations. I do not control others even when it is appropriate. I do not, for example, take charge even during a fire in a children's schoolhouse in which I am the only adult. I never make a decision if I can refer it to someone else. In a bureaucracy, I follow the "cover your ass" philosophy.

When I am an *autocrat*, I am dominating in the extreme. I am a power-seeker, a competitor. I am afraid that others will not be influenced by me, that they will in fact dominate me. My underlying feeling is the same as that of the abdicrat; I am not capable of discharging obligation. To compensate for this feeling, I try to keep proving that I am capable, with the result that I take on too much responsibility.

When I am a *democrat*, that is, when in my childhood I successfully resolved my relations in the control area, power and control present no problem. I feel comfortable giving or not giving orders, taking or not taking orders, whichever is appropriate to the situation. Unlike the abdicrat and the autocrat, I am not preoccupied with fears of my own helplessness, stupidity, or incompetence. I feel competent, and I am confident that other people trust my ability to make decisions.

The problem of control is *top or bottom*. The primary control interaction is *confrontation*. The control anxiety is that I am *incompetent*.

## AFFECTION

Affection behavior describes close, personal, emotional feelings between two people. Affection is a dyadic relation; that is, it occurs between pairs of people, whereas both inclusion and control relations may occur either in dyads or between one person and a group of persons.

Since affection is based on building emotional ties, it is usually the last phase to emerge in the development of a human relation or of a group. In the inclusion phase, people encounter each other and decide whether to continue their relation; control issues lead them to confront one another and to work out how they will relate. As the relation continues, if affection ties form, people literally or figuratively embrace.

Underlying my behavior in the affection area is my feeling of lovability. If I do not feel lovable, if I feel like a nasty, evil, obnoxious person who would be rejected by anyone who knows me well, then my affection behavior is extreme and anxious. Either I avoid all close, emotional ties, the underpersonal, or I keep trying to get close to everyone, the overpersonal.

When I am *underpersonal*, I avoid close ties with others. I maintain one-to-one relations on a superficial, distant level and I am most comfortable when other people do the same with me. I maintain emotional distance and I do not become emotionally involved. Unconsciously, I seek a satisfactory affectional relation. My fear is that no one loves me, and that I will not be liked. I have great difficulty genuinely liking people, and I distrust their feelings toward me.

My attitude is: "I find the affection area very painful since I have been rejected; therefore, I shall avoid close personal relations in the future." My direct technique as an underpersonal is to avoid emotional closeness or involvement, even to the point of being antagonistic. My subtle technique is to be superficially friendly to everyone, even to the point of being "popular," which acts as a safeguard against becoming especially close to any one person.

When I am an *overpersonal*, I become extremely close to others, and I want others to be close to me. The unaware feeling on which I operate is: "My first experiences with affection were painful, but perhaps if I try again, they will turn out to be better." Being liked is essential to my attempt to relieve anxiety about being rejected and unloved. My direct technique for being liked is to attempt to gain approval, to be extremely personal, ingratiating, intimate, and confiding. My subtle technique, more manipulative and possessive, is to devour friends and to punish any attempts by them to establish other friendships.

When I am a *personal*, one who successfully resolved affection relations in childhood, close emotional interaction with another person presents no problem. I am comfortable in a close personal relation as well as in a situation requiring emotional distance. It is important for me to be liked, but if I am not, I can accept that the dislike is the result of the relation between me and the other person; in other words, the dislike does not mean that I am an unlovable person. I am capable of giving and taking genuine affection.

The primary interaction of the affection area is the expression of appropriate deeper feelings. At the beginning of a group, there are many statements about how difficult it is to express hostility to people. Most people are surprised to find that it is even more difficult to express warm, positive feelings.

With respect to interpersonal relations, inclusion is concerned with relations already formed. Within existent relations, control is the area concerned with who gives orders and makes decisions, whereas affection is concerned with how emotionally close or distant the relation becomes.

The problem of affection is *near or far*. The affection interaction is *embrace*. The affection anxiety is that I am *unlovable*.

## GROUP DEVELOPMENT

These three dimensions—inclusion, control, and affection—occur, in that order, in the development of a group. Inclusion issues, the decision to be in or out of the group, arise first, followed by control issues (top or bottom), and, finally, by affection issues (near or far). This order is not rigid, but the nature of group life is such that people tend first to determine whether they want to be in a group, then to find out what place of influence they will occupy, and finally to decide how personally close they will become.

### INCLUSION PHASE

The inclusion phase of group development begins at the formation of the group. As a member of a new group, I want first to find where I fit. My first concerns are to decide whether I want to be in or out of the group, to establish myself as a specific individual, and to see if I am going to be paid attention to or to be ignored. When I am anxious about these issues, I tend toward individual-centered behavior—overtalking, extreme withdrawal, exhibitionism, or recitation of my biography.

At the same time, I am deciding to what degree I will commit myself to this group—how much investment I will withdraw from my other life commitments to invest in this new relation. I am asking, "How much of myself will I give to this group? How important will I be in this setting? Will they appreciate who I am and what I can do, or will I be indistinguishable from many others?" This is the problem of identity. I am primarily deciding how much contact, interaction, and communication I wish to have.

During this process of group formation, my main concerns are the issues of crossing or not crossing the boundaries of the group, and of belonging or not belonging to that group. Boundary issues are problems of inclusion.

Characteristic of groups in this phase is the appearance of "goblet issues."[53] This term is taken from cocktail party behavior where people sometimes pick up their cocktail glass, or goblet, peer through it, and size up the other people at the party. Goblet issues are those which, in themselves, are of minor importance to the group members but which function as vehicles for getting to know one another. A goblet issue is often made of the first decision confronting a group.

The goblet issue is by no means confined to cocktail parties. Each group finds its own goblet issues within its own framework. "The weather" is universal; "rules of procedure" is common in formal groups; "Do you know . . . ?" is characteristic for acquaintances from the same locale; relating incidents or telling stories has a goblet element for business gatherings; and "Where are you from?" serves in military settings. On college campuses straights ask "What's your major?", hip students start with, "Ever take acid?"

Although discussions of these topics are often pointless in content, through them members usually learn much about one another. As a group member, I know better who responds favorably to me, who sees things the way I do, how intelligent I am compared to the others, and how the group leader reacts to me. I also have some idea of the type of role I can expect to play in the group.

Contrary to outward appearances, such discussions are inevitable, and they do serve an important function. Groups not permitted this type of testing will search for some other method of obtaining the same information, perhaps using a decision of more importance to the group.

## CONTROL PHASE

Once the sense of being together in a group is somewhat established, control issues become prominent. Control issues include decision-making, sharing responsibility, and the distribution of power. During the control stage, characteristic group behavior includes a struggle for leadership and competition. As a group member, at this point, my primary anxieties center on having too much or too little responsibility, and too much or too little influence. I try to establish myself in the group in such a way that I will have the amount of power and dependency most comfortable for me.

### AFFECTION PHASE

Following some resolution of the issue of control, affection issues take center stage. Individuals have come together to form a group. They have differentiated themselves with respect to responsibility and power. Now they explore the issue of becoming emotionally integrated. At this stage, it is characteristic to see expressions of positive feeling, direct personal hostility, jealousy, pairing off, and, in general, heightened emotional feeling between pairs of people.

As a group member, my primary anxieties focus on not being liked, on not being close enough to people, and on being too intimate. I am striving to obtain the most comfortable amount of affectional exchange and the most comfortable position in regard to initiating and receiving affection. Like Schopenhauer's porcupines, which had the problem of huddling together on a cold night, I want to get close enough to receive warmth yet stay far enough away to avoid the pain of sharp quills.

### CYCLING

The group development hypothesis asserts that certain interactional areas are emphasized at certain points in a group's growth. All three areas are always present but not always equally salient. Similarly, some persons do not always go along with the central issue for the group. For certain individuals, a particular dimension will be so personally potent that it will transcend the current group issue. For each person, the area of concern at any one time is the resultant of the problem areas of the individual and those of the group's current phase.

The cycling of developmental phases is analogous to changing tires. When a mechanic changes a tire and replaces the wheel, each bolt is tightened just enough to keep the wheel in place. Then the bolts are tightened further, usually in the same sequence, until the wheel is firmly in place. Finally, each bolt is gone over separately to secure it fast. Like these bolts, the three areas are worked on until they have been resolved sufficiently to allow the group to continue with the work at hand. Later, each area is returned to and is worked on until it is more satisfactorily resolved. If one bolt is not tightened well in the first cycle, during the next cycle it receives more attention.

Since all groups are comprised of members with interpersonal desires, this theory of group development applies to any interpersonal relation. Every time people form themselves into groups, including two-person groups, the same three interpersonal areas are dealt with in the same order. In certain social situations, external forces may be imposed to alter the manner of handling these areas, but they still must be dealt with.

In a military organization, the uniform helps to create a feeling of belonging, or inclusion. The stripes or bars on the arm or shoulder clarify the issues of control and power distribution. Fraternization rules and customs influence the expression of affection. These external factors by no means solve the interpersonal problems, however. Uniformed soldiers may still feel they are being ignored as individuals or that they are not being treated as important persons. Sergeants may feel they should have more influence than their inexperienced lieutenants. A captain may feel that the rules of personal separation for officers and enlisted personnel conflict with the desire to become more intimate with a corporal.

## SEPARATION

As groups terminate, they resolve their relations in the opposite sequence, namely, affection, control, and inclusion. Groups or relations that are about to finish or to markedly reduce their interaction exhibit characteristic behaviors: absences and latenesses increase; there is more daydreaming; members forget to bring materials to the group; discussion of death and illness is frequent; the importance and goodness of the group is minimized; general involvement decreases.

Often there is recall of earlier experiences. As a member of a terminating group, I usually want to discuss with the group the events that were not completely worked through at the time they occurred— the incomplete energy cycles. In this way, I hope my relations will be resolved successfully. Often, when I feel that my actions in an earlier meeting were misunderstood, I will recall the instance and explain what I really meant to say, so no one will be angry with me. Sometimes, I want to express to other members that comments they made earlier were important to me. On it goes, with all unresolved incidents being reworked. After the group members complete this process of reworking unresolved incidents, we are readier to accept separation.

In the process of group resolution, the personal, positive, and negative feelings are dealt with first (affection). Next, the discussion focuses on the leader and on the reasons for compliance with, or rebellion against, the leader's wishes (control). Later come discussions about the possibilities of continuing the group and about how committed each member really was, and, finally, about the fact that the group members are going in different directions and will no longer be members of the present group (inclusion).

My responses to impending separation depend upon my major areas of desire and on my preferred methods of coping with anxiety. As a group member, I may respond to impending separation by gradually withdrawing my investment in the group as indicated by my increased absence, lateness, and reduced participation. Or I may disparage and demean the group, as if to say: "You see, I won't miss such an unimportant group." Or I may shift the responsibility for separation onto the other group members by becoming antagonistic and forcing them to reject me. Or separation may be so difficult for me that my method of handling it has become a character trait: I refrain from becoming invested in people from the first time I meet them.

## CHOOSING A SPECIFIC ILLNESS

The dimensions of Inclusion, Control, and Affection provide the means for understanding why I choose one illness rather than another.

As mentioned above, every disease is the result of an out-of-awareness conflict that is, literally, "embodied." Any illness is an expression of a total life situation. It is my attempt to cope with my life situation. Often being ill allows me to quit work, to take a rest, to avoid responsibility, to postpone deadlines, to be waited on, and to be given sympathy, flowers, and bon bons. Specific illnesses have special benefits.

Different organ systems in my body are specifically appropriate to deal with the relations between me and the outside world and also to deal with my different parts. An understanding of which body parts correspond to the functions of inclusion, control, and affection will illuminate the reason for my selection of specific diseases.

### INCLUSION ILLNESS

On the physical level, inclusion refers to the boundaries between myself and the rest of the world, and therefore deals primarily with the periphery of my body—the skin, the sense organs, eyes, ears, nose, and mouth—and the systems of the body that exchange with the environment: the respiratory system, that takes in and gives out air, the digestive-excretory system, that exchanges food with the environment. Attitudes toward these organs are related to my attitudes toward being included by others.

Illness of the skin, senses, respiration, or digestion-excretion are expressions of out-of-awareness conflicts about inclusion. If I am unconsciously conflicted about inclusion, I may develop hives or acne or shingles or rashes. This keeps people away from me.

If I am uncomfortable being in close proximity to people, I may not see them clearly until they are ten feet away. We call that far sighted. Or, if I am comfortable with close friends but afraid of strangers, I may see things clearly up to a few feet away and then see only a blur, that is, I become myopic.

If I do not want to hear what people have to say I will make myself deaf. Many deaf people did not listen before they became deaf.

Bioenergetics practitioners have observed that if I do not feel significant (inclusion) as a child, I fail to inhale the normal amount of air. My chest becomes too narrow, my rib cage is small, and I am more susceptible to respiratory illnesses because I do not breathe fully. If I am anxious that if I exhale I may never get another breath, my rib cage is too deep. I am barrel-chested. I do not really believe that I can relax and breathe normally and remain included.

Eating has an inclusion element to it. Too little or too much food carries an implication of caring and being paid attention to. There is also a control element present in digestion, especially with regard to the power struggle around "eating everything on your plate" and especially when excretion and toilet training become involved. Diseases of digestion and excretion represent a transition between problems of inclusion and problems of control.

Cancer is primarily an inclusion disease, although the location of the cancer is also significant. The work of the Simontons[4] on cancer patients described on page 165 is based on a holistic philosophy very similar to that presented here. They assume that cancer is a manifestation of the total organism and they treat it from that standpoint.

The Simontons have used FIRO-B,[51] an instrument to measure the cancer patient's characteristic behavior in the areas of inclusion, control, and affection. The interesting differences between their cancer patients and people in the general population occur primarily in the inclusion area. The still living patients score extremely low on wanting to be included in activities with other people. They have little desire to be in a group but rely on their own resources.

The general sense of the traditional, that is, non-Simonton, cancer patient is of one who has given up, who has opted out of this life. Sometimes it appears that they have a strong will to live, but there is probably a strong unconscious part of them that wishes to die. Inferences could be made about public figures who contracted cancer and died quickly after an event that could be interpreted as existentially terminal. For example, Senator Joe McCarthy died of cancer shortly after being censured by his Senate colleagues and losing his power, and Hubert Humphrey died shortly after he lost his final bid to become president.

## CONTROL ILLNESS

The organ systems I use to control my body are the muscles and skeleton, the nervous system, and the endocrines. These are the systems that I use to cope with the world, to keep myself safe, and to assert myself.

When I embody an out-of-awareness conflict about control, I give myself a disease of these systems. The interpretation of arthritis as holding back anger, especially arthritis of the hands and legs, is well documented.[54] Often young people, especially girls, will wish to hit their mother but be prevented by guilt and fear. When this guilt becomes overwhelming, the arthritis is a way to prevent themselves physically from striking out.

Diseases of the nervous system have not yet been studied extensively from this standpoint, but several pieces of data are indicative. Spinal cord injuries typically occur in males aged 16 to 28 usually as a result of auto, motorcycle, or diving accidents. The establishment of the macho image for young men is a central feature of the control area. It is not a large inferential leap to assume that these men had an unconscious conflict in the area of masculinity and achievement that was expressed through their "accidents." One man told me that his "accident" had taken him out of the macho race, to his great relief.

I have found agreement among several nurses who worked with spinal patients that these patients are typically difficult to handle.

It is well known among these nurses that amyotropic lateral sclerosis (Lou Gehrig's disease) patients, for example, are typically rebellious and generally dominate the nurses' attention.

Headaches are a milder form of nervous disorder. Appropriate research is lacking, but clinical observation indicates that I get headaches when I feel incompetent. They often occur when I am about to go to a meeting unprepared, or when there is so much going on that I do not understand what is happening.

## AFFECTION ILLNESS

Affection is expressed in the body through love, the heart, and sex, the genitals. The circulatory system is an expression of the state of affection as recognized by the vernacular: "broken-hearted," "I open my heart to you," "sweetheart." A report of an Israeli study concluded that: "There seems to be a direct correlation between your wife's love and support and that heart of yours—the physical heart, that is . . . And how your boss feels about you also plays a role. The higher the appreciation, the less risk of a heart attack."[55]

In another study[56] Stewart Wolf of St. Lukes Hospital in Bethlehem, Pennsylvania, demonstrated a direct relation between the climbing rate of heart attacks and the loss of community closeness over a fifteen year period.

The town of Roseto, Pennsylvania, became moderately famous in the early 1960s when it was discovered that its inhabitants had a remarkably low death rate, especially from heart attacks. Since they tended toward obesity and did not differ appreciably from neighboring populations in other factors associated with heart disease (smoking, fat consumption, lack of exercise, serum cholesterol levels), the researchers speculated that social factors might be the key.

The townspeople were predominantly Italian-Americans whose ancestors had been forced into an insular, close community. They were involved in each other's lives, honored the elderly, supported each other strongly in times of personal crisis. Wolf said, "This was more than ethnicity—they developed such a cohesive, mutually supportive society that no one was ever abandoned."

He and his fellow investigators predicted in 1963 that the Rosetans would begin reflecting more typical patterns of heart attacks and other diseases as their life style was Americanized. That is just what has happened. There has been a striking increase in death rates, most notably in men under 55.

By the mid-1960s younger Rosetans had begun to resent social isolation and clannishness. They began to marry non-Italians, joined country clubs, bought Cadillacs and ranch houses, changed churches or quit going to church. Tradition and community closeness declined.

"For the first time," Wolf said, "young men are dying of myocardial infarction," a killer known to be strikingly less prevalent in those parts of the world where tradition and family ties are strong.

The relation of the heart and of the circulatory system to affection may also account for the engulfing quality of a love relation. When love is good, all the world is right; when love is bad or absent, nothing seems to work. Blood circulation nourishes the whole body. If it is constricted, the entire organism has difficulty getting sufficient nourishment. If blood flows freely through a relaxed and open heart, the whole self is well fed.

Genital ailments, such as vaginitis and herpes, as well as syphilis and gonorrhea often occur at embarrassing moments. The present theory asserts that they occur when there is some out-of-awareness conflict over love, particularly the sexual aspect of love. If there is sexual guilt, if infidelity is an issue, if religious or social mores are being violated, and if I am not letting myself be aware of my conflict, that is the time I am most likely to get genital illnesses.

## SEX

Sexual expression is primarily an affection function although various aspects of the sexual act parallel inclusion and control.

Inclusion problems refer to the initial phases of intercourse, feelings about penetration. If I were a male with unaware problems of inclusion, I would probably have *potency* difficulties. My conflict over whether to penetrate would be reflected in the enervation of my penis and its unwillingness to enter. If I were a woman with inclusion problems, my tight, dry vagina would express my unwillingness to receive a penis.

When I was uncertain as to whether I wanted to be married, I had problems with erection. As that conflict became resolved, so did my potency problems. The sexual problem manifested my feeling about the whole relationship.

The control aspect of the sexual act centers on *orgasm*. Orgasm timing expresses control and willingness to surrender. I may withhold orgasm in an attempt to make it easy for you to feel unsatisfactory as a sexual satisfier. I may come quickly and create conditions within which you will find it more difficult to have an orgasm. I may try to direct your physical movement, or to let you do the moving, as an expression of our power relations to each other. When a relation is in its control phase, orgasm is usually the area of sexual difficulty. When the control problem is clarified, the orgasm problem is alleviated.

The affection aspect of the sexual act is the *feeling* that follows completion of intercourse. This feeling may be anything from a flood of warm, affectionate, loving feelings to revulsion and thoughts such as: "What am I doing here?" or, "No, I won't take you to breakfast." The feeling depends partly on how well the heart and genitals are connected. Affection is the aspect of sex that is much better when there is a deep love between the partners.

This analysis helps to clarify a phenomenon puzzling to many: "If I love her (or him) so much, how come I sometimes find someone else a better sex partner? Maybe I'm not really in love."

Not at all. A casual sexual encounter, even a one-nighter, where there are no problems of inclusion or control in the relationship, that is, when both partners are clear that they want to be together and there is no power struggle, may result in a splendid sexual experience. The sexual problem occurs after the sexual performance is completed, at the point of feeling. Here is where the undeveloped emotional nature of the relationship becomes evident. But the actual sexual contact may be highly successful without calling into question the depth of the primary relationship.

## CHILDHOOD

Because the dimensions of inclusion, control, and affection are assumed to exist from conception onward, they should be detectable in the early years. In an earlier publication,[57] I reviewed the literature on parent-child relations and concluded that studies in that area also depended on the three dimensions. Different investigators used different terms, but most emerged with three factors that were quite similar to inclusion, control, and affection.

In these studies, inclusion is also called parent-child interaction, stimulation, and, in the extreme, indulgence. High inclusion in parent-child relations is characterized by a child-centered home with the child constantly subject to attention, concern, action, and a high level of activity. Intense and frequent contact with both parents is the norm. Low inclusion is characterized by an adult-centered home where the child is left to its own devices, neglected, ignored, and understimulated. Interaction with parents is low even for spankings, and the child is not paid any attention even when committing such disapproved activities as neglect of chores, disobedience, and masturbation.

In the context of parent-child relations, control is also called democracy and promotion of independence. The low end of control includes freedom to choose, decide, originate, and reject—freedom from arbitrary control in general. Parents typically justify their policies, decide democratically, explain readily, answer the child's questions about sex, take the child on picnics, give spending money, and do not interfere in the child's fights. High control shows the child restrained strictly within the bounds of autocratic despotism, obedience is demanded, suggestions are given coercively, and regulations are restrictive.

In these studies, affection is also called affectionateness, approval, and acceptance of the child. High control includes behavior that is affectionate, accepting, approving, encouraging, and facilitating. Low affection shows the child blamed, discouraged, disapproved, rejected, and inhibited as well as not receiving affection.

Reinforcing the importance of these areas of interaction is the Gluecks's classic study[58] of delinquency, which resulted in the same finding. The authors had considerable success in predicting which children would eventually be delinquent by using these factors: cohesiveness of the family (inclusion), discipline by the father and supervision by the mother (control), and affection of the father and of the mother (affection).

## PSYCHOANALYSTS

One way to reconcile the differences between the three major early psychoanalytic figures, Freud, Adler, and Jung, is to relate them to the dimensions of inclusion, control, and affection. Perhaps each of these theorists saw most clearly one of the three dimensions and made that dimension his central concern.

The keystone for Freud was the libido—sexual energy—and its expression and sublimation. This was the chief theoretical point at which both Adler and Jung departed. In my terms, sexual energy is most prominent in the affection area, although, of course, it has effects in the other two areas as well.

Adler chose to focus his theory on the will to power. Clearly, he was emphasizing the control area, the dimension that deals with power, authority, and competition.

Jung's core concept is our relation to nature. He was concerned with mysticism and archetypes that show our continuity with the universe. His primary psychological dimension was introversion-extroversion, almost identical with in-out, or the inclusion dimension.

All three men had ways of accounting for phenomena in the other two areas. Their differences may be clarified by considering that each felt that a different one of the three dimensions was central: for Freud, affection; for Adler, control; for Jung, inclusion.

## I-NATURE

I offer another speculation, both for its own intrinsic interest and to expand the theory to larger units, such as people in nature, much as it has been expanded to smaller units, such as the body.

Assume that we relate to the natural world along the same dimensions that we do to each other. How then do we relate to nature in the areas of inclusion, control, and affection?

Inclusion issues address the fundamental relation of myself to nature. Do I want to include myself in nature? Do I want to live or die? What role do I play in nature? Am I a mere speck in the universe or am I one with the cosmos? What is my importance, my significance, my commitment to life? How worthwhile is it for me to stay in the natural world? The institutions that we have created to deal with these issues we call *religion* and mysticism.

My control relation to nature involves establishing my influence over the forces of nature and my dependence on the natural world for survival. I build dwellings for protection from the weather, and I invent ways to alter nature, to extract materials from the earth, and to produce heat, light, and food. To succeed in this quest, I must understand nature, learn to overcome natural difficulties, and use nature's resources. The institutions created to deal with these issues we call *science* and engineering.

Expressing my feelings toward nature in the affection area involves uniting very personal expressions of union and harmony (or the opposite) with natural phenomena. Sometimes, this expression is direct, as when, as an architect, I attempt to harmonize structures with their natural settings, or, as an artist, I express my perceptions of a landscape, or, as a sculptor, I take materials from the earth and fashion them in my own unique way. This is a one-to-one relation, like the interpersonal aspect of affection, and unlike the bulk of science, which is necessarily a cumulative enterprise. This individualistic self-expression we institutionalize as *art*.

The institutions established for expressing our relation to nature in the areas of inclusion, control, and affection are religion, science, and art.

# I-THOU

If we look at the social patterns we establish to regulate our relations with each other in the areas of inclusion, control, and affection, we should find cultural institutions that have arisen to deal with these three issues.

The inclusion area is the one least clear. Attempts to devise institutions through which we can contact each other, avoid loneliness, and experience each other's company are exemplified by fraternal and sororal organizations, mixers, and encounter groups. Organizations such as the Elks and Rotary frequently exist for a long time without a specified goal. The Shriners, for example, existed for several decades before they chose to support hospitals as a group function. It appeared that they had selected an outside activity to justify their existence, thereby allowing them to continue to satisfy their original desire to be together.

The social institutions we establish to regulate our relations in the control area are much more elaborate. Politics, economics, and the military are institutions concerned with the exercise and distribution of power in legal, financial, and martial forms. It is striking how much more developed are our institutions for dealing with control than are those for dealing with inclusion.

The social patterns we establish to regulate our relations in the affection area center around the institution of marriage. Marriage consists of an elaborate set of conventions specifying the ways in which one-to-one affectional relations are to be expressed. Due to the apparent inadequacy of this one pattern to accommodate all human possibilities, many alternatives to marriage have evolved, and the institution itself has come upon hard times. Attempts to deal with the affection problem are exacerbated by the law which makes the acceptable patterns of affection difficult to alter. Our culture has only begun to acknowledge the legitimacy of homosexual affection. The gay liberation movement and requests for homosexual marriages have focused attention on these issues.

In summary, our culture has established the institutions of fraternal and sororal organizations for inclusion; economics, politics, and the military for control; and marriage for affection. The institutions established to deal with issues of control and of heterosexual affection are the most fully developed. Less developed are the institutions that deal with homosexual affection and with inclusion. This suggests where we are in our development as a civilization and what kind of institutions must evolve if we are to provide institutionally for the basic human dimensions.

*The table below provides a summary of the various expressions of inclusion, control, and affection.*

| Issue | INCLUSION | CONTROL | AFFECTION |
|---|---|---|---|
| | In or Out | Top or Bottom | Near or Far |
| Interaction | Encounter | Confront | Embrace |
| Self-Concept | Significance | Competence | Lovability |
| Body Level | Energy | Integration | Acceptance |
| Sexual Response | Potency | Orgasm | Feeling |
| Physiology (System) | Senses | Nervous | Reproductive |
| | Respiratory | Muscular | Circulatory |
| | Digestive | Skeletal | |
| | Excretory | Endocrine | |
| Extreme Illness | Cancer | Spinal Disease | Heart Trouble |
| Parent-Child Relation | Interaction | Independence | Acceptance |
| Psychoanalytic Theorist | Jung | Adler | Freud |
| I-Nature | Religion | Science | Art |
| I-Thou | Fraternal and Sororal Organizations | Politics | Marriage |
| | | Economics | |
| | | Military | |

# 2

## APPLICATIONS

> I do not think that the United States civilization of these last 40–50 years is a successful civilization. I think this country is destined to succumb to failures which cannot be other than tragic and enormous in their scope. . . . This society bears the seeds of its own horrors—unbreathable air, undrinkable water, starvation. . . . We have nothing to teach the world. We have to confess that we have not got the answers to the problems of human society in the modern age.
>
> —George Kennan[59]

Many signposts indicate a growing recognition that our social institutions, now based largely on principles opposite to those being presented here, are not working well. When it comes to people, either as individuals or in groups, our progress has been paltry because our basis is shaky. Division of persons into mind and body, social patina and hypocrisy substituting for honesty, massive confusion over responsibility, and a public collusion to flee from self-awareness have led us to what is at best an impasse and at worst terminal illness.

Unemployment does not decline, cancer research is not successful, crime rises, life expectancy after childhood has not risen in years, psychology doubts itself, and organizations do not change. Watergate indignation passes, no significant laws are enacted, and corruption begins anew. Outrage over assassinations fades, no new laws are made, and terrorism and frustration resume. Nothing fundamental is happening. Our superficial solutions, that is, those that do not address themselves to changes in people, lead only to repetition.

"Social psychologists once knew who they were and where they were going. . . . Exciting new research discoveries were often reported and theoretical developments seemed to promise dramatic advances in the understanding of human behavior. . . . During the past decade . . . many social psychologists appear to have lost not only their faith in the discipline's future. . . . Most seem agreed that a crisis is at hand."[60]

"Despite soaring outlays in the war against crime, lawlessness in America is not likely to be reduced substantially for at least the next five to ten years, the director of the federal anti-crime research program says."[61]

"This is a book that describes a distinguished failure in organizational development (OD) . . . This OD experience was stacked in favor of succeeding . . . yet the project failed . . . Argyris' book will be a landmark as the account of one of the great failures of applied social science if it results in the needed reappraisal of the intellectual and scientific underpinnings of the OD field. This optimistic outcome is not assured, however, since individuals may also be characterized by 'self-sealing, non-learning processes' . . . just as Argyris claims that organizations are."[62]

In medicine, several books and articles (typified by one such title: The End of Medicine[63]) are exposing the inadequacies of the profession of medicine. The ineffectiveness of the prison system for either deterrence or rehabilitation is being faced (typified, not coincidentally, by the parallel title The End of Imprisonment[64]). The inequities of the tax laws, the overburdened, cumbersome, and biased court system, the retreat from religion, the sorry reading scores of high school graduates, the frequent paralyses from labor turmoil, and the conversion of athletic magnificence into an arena for political strife and financial greed are events widely viewed with dismay.

Not that these situations are necessarily worse than

they have ever been, but spurred by the revelations regarding Watergate, the Vietnam War, and the CIA-FBI peccadillos, our awareness of the lack in our institutions has increased. Increased awareness is a legacy of the revolutions of the sixties with their demands for an end to sophistry.

The principles of profound simplicity afford a basis for transforming institutions toward a consistent social philosophy, a philosophy that begins with the nature of the human organism and constructs society around that. These principles could lead to the kind of long-needed evolution in human interaction which would equal advances in material technology.

# PRINCIPLES OF APPLICATION

Following is a conversion of the principles of profound simplicity into a guide for applying these principles.

## GOAL

*The aim of any social institution is the creation of social conditions within which individuals choose to find it easiest to determine their own lives.*

This goal is accomplished by removing obstacles to self-determination and by creating circumstances that encourage self-awareness.

## FREEDOM

*Permit any action done by an individual, with awareness, that does not impinge on another individual.*

## AGREEMENT

*Allow any action between two or more people, done with awareness by both, that does not impinge on others.*

Minimize the role of outside determiners, such as laws, judges, and referees. In the ultimate, when everyone is fully aware, there is no need for laws. All events are agreements.

## TRUTH

*By eliminating dishonesty, create conditions that make awareness easier.*

At this time, it is often impractical for a person to determine the honesty of another individual, such as a salesman or a professional practitioner. An institution may help assure that statements made by such people are accurate and that each person does not have to spend much time and energy determining credentials, experience, product quality, and so on.

## SIMPLICITY

*Provide profoundly simple solutions to problems that individuals choose to have dealt with by institutions.*

When a problem (like traffic or welfare) has a complex solution it is because we do not yet understand it very well. Profoundly simple solutions deepen understanding of the problem and free energy for other areas of life. Simple solutions are easier to understand, therefore enhance self-determination since people do not have to comprehend enormous complexity, as exists, for example, in the present tax laws.

## CHOICE

*Create conditions within which individuals choose to find it easier to realize that they choose their own lives.*

When people do not allow themselves to know this, they block themselves from self-determination.

## OPTIONS

*Create conditions within which people choose to find it easy to become aware of options.*

If I do not let myself know that other possibilities exist, I block my self-determination. Awareness may be created, for example, through education, some types of advertising, and alternative forms of medicine.

## SELF-RESPONSIBILITY

*Reward self-responsibility.*

It is a great deterrent to self-determination when the law accepts a defense such as: "I wasn't responsible for what I did. I was just following orders." This encourages blaming and dependency and discourages independence. (Who chose to follow orders?)

## AWARENESS

*Reward awareness.*

When a person is relieved of responsibility because "I didn't know what I was doing," lack of awareness and self-deception are encouraged and being aware is discouraged. (Who chose to be unaware?)

## TRANSITION

*Provide for a minimal delay in changing social practices to allow the unaware person to become aware and to make a conscious choice.*

The delay is solely for the purpose of supporting a transition to the point of self-determination and must occur for a limited time only. If the unaware person chooses to remain unaware, the delay is terminated.

This principle does not follow obviously from what has already been presented, but is introduced because most of us are not very honest, do not have great awareness, and do not realize that we are choosing our own lives.

Immediate replacement of current social practices with a distortion of those described here might be used to justify such undesirable outcomes as the sanctioning of murder and rape and the abandonment of accident victims since all participants in such events may be considered to be colluders.

Thus, a reasonable method for effecting the transition must be considered carefully. The fact that this transition is an issue underscores one of the chief purposes of social institutions—to provide individuals time to become aware of their unaware choices. An equally important institutional function is to support self-determination. These two purposes require a sensitive balance expressed through a delay to provide time—time that is kept minimal to support self-determination.

This balance is a keystone of political philosophy. A traditional difference between the two American political parties may be clarified through this concept.

The Democratic tradition is to use the government to support those segments of the society which are poor, handicapped, or apparently unable to help themselves. The Democrats are constantly vulnerable to the criticism that they spend too much money.

The Republican focus, theoretically, is on "a more limited government with primary responsibility as close to the people as possible . . . individual freedom and self-reliance—many of the old virtues—must be preserved."[65] The way the Republicans have implemented this principle has led them, in the eyes of one of their own leaders,[66] to be "regarded by many as hard, callous, cruel and insensitive."

Those criticisms are at least partly correct. The Democrats understand the need for supporting people who are not choosing to support themselves. But the Democrats are not sufficiently clear that such support, to be most valuable, must be for a limited period. Exceeding a limited time indicates their actions are not supporting individual self-determination; they are supporting individual dependency. Therefore, the government goes on spending and the budget goes awry.

The Republicans, on the other hand, appreciate the end result of self-reliance, but they are not sufficiently sensitive to the fact that many people have not let themselves be oriented in that direction. Their programs do not provide sufficient support for such people to right themselves and to step onto the path toward self-reliance. In that sense, they are insensitive and as a result, their policies are often callous and cruel.

These dilemmas are resolved when an institution chooses to support those people who are not allowing themselves to be aware, by providing them with the time to become aware while simultaneously making clear (by providing information and knowledge of options) that this support is temporary and solely for the purpose of easing the way to self-determination.

In this way, the institution avoids both the criticism of Democratic profligacy and paternalism and the criticism of Republican callousness and cruelty. This minimal delay and support provides the path for the transition between our present situation and the one envisioned through the principles of profound simplicity.

In many social institutions, medicine and education, for example, these principles of application provide theoretical support for already existing trends. For other areas, in particular law and athletics, they suggest some radical though not unprecedented innovations. I shall now present a few specific suggestions for various institutional changes derived from the above principles.

# LAW

Social institutions reward unawareness. If I am not aware that I make myself sick, I am given sick leave and health benefits. If I am aware that I make myself sick, I keep myself healthy and I work more. If I am not aware that I contribute to being a victim, I receive the benefits of the law and the sympathy of society. If I am aware, I either do not allow myself to be victimized, or I acknowledge complicity and reject rewards. If I am not aware that I choose poverty, I receive welfare and assistance. If I am aware, I make it on my own. Society rewards the ill, the victim, and the indigent.

In the Western World, the more pervasive the sickness, the richer the doctors. Hospitals go out of business if their beds are not filled or if patients do not stay long enough. The greatest economic tragedy that could befall Western medicine is the total health of the citizenry.

In the East, the old acupuncturists were paid when their patients were well. They would examine and balance their patients at the beginning of each season, four times a year. Acupuncturists were paid as long as their patients stayed well. If a patient became ill, the acupuncturist would support the patient and the patient's family for the duration of the illness. For the acupuncturists, the greatest economic bonanza occurred when all patients remained healthy.

We could structure our social programs so that we rewarded pro-life forces such as health, independence, and self-sufficiency rather than their opposites. Rewarding awareness makes it more difficult for most people to remain unaware. If I receive no social support or sympathy for being a victim, I must either be content with that reaction or I must become more aware of my contribution to being a victim.

But what if I choose not to be aware? Do I not have a right to be unaware if I choose to? Of course, I have a right to be unaware, but I do not have a right to demand rewards from society for choosing to be unaware.

What about the situation where one person is harmed by another, physically beaten, or robbed? What is the responsibility of the aggressor? Is there no such thing as "right thinking" or morality? Yes, I suspect there is. The problem is: How is it to be determined?

Let us start at the origin. A strong person hits a weak one. Both have colluded, at some level of their awarenesses, to bring about this event. Supposing I, the weak one, do not like what happened. I have not let myself be aware of the part of me that colluded to bring about my pummeling. If I allow myself to become aware of that part, I may find that I feel guilt over some early event in my life and that my latent masochism leads me to taunt bullies. I may find that my weaker brother got all the attention, and I wanted to elicit sympathy the way he did by putting myself in a situation where I am aggressed against. Becoming aware, I might decide that I no longer want to get beaten up, and I might stop taunting, learn judo, avoid bullies, make friends with bullies, or engage the services of two bodyguards.

If I am not yet in contact with the part of me that wanted the beating, and if I knew that I awarely wanted to avoid it, I might appeal to others, or to laws, to prevent a recurrence of the mayhem until I come to full awareness and am willing to cope with the situation myself. I invoke the principle of transition.

The function of the law is to prevent my colluding, on a level of which I am not aware, with someone to bring about an activity I feel I would not want to participate in if I were fully aware. Murder, robbery, and rape are some obvious examples.

The stronger person may be quite pleased with the situation and not motivated to change his or her behavior. But this is not "right thinking." Is there not some morality that should come from within the person to govern his or her behavior? Perhaps, but how do we determine right thinking? If the judgment as to what is right thinking is subjective, the problem remains. Hitler had a splendid rationale for his actions.

A better solution is to stay with the principle of self-responsibility and to avoid the route of absolute morality. If you, the stronger, find that other people do not associate with you, do not approve of you, do not vote for you, do not patronize your store or purchase your services as a result of your hitting the weaker, you may change your behavior. If you find that someone hits you in return, you also may change your behavior one way or the other. If you find that a majority of people, society, have decided that your behavior should lead you to be incarcerated, you may be affected. You are then confronted with the consequences of your behavior, and you would probably then make a new choice. This all occurs without the necessity of an external code of morality.

Some of these reactions of other people to you, the stronger, may help you become more aware. You may discover an old frustration at your inability to combat your father, which you are venting on a weaker person. You may discover a feeling of sexual inadequacy, which you are attempting to compensate for by being macho. Or you may have been jealous of a sibling for getting more attention than you did. As you become more aware, you have a wider range of options for your next behavior.

You are also developing a sense of yourself and of the type of person you want to be. Since your self-concept is your choice, you may decide to be any kind of person you choose. The self-concept becomes an alternative to a moral code. You may decide, for example, that you wish to be a person who is thoughtful or helpful or nonviolent. Creating your behavior consistent with that image is a strong determinant of your behavior. Typically, this is more effective than a social code of morality because you have generated the image as a result of your own personal experience, and you have chosen to conform to it. It has not been imposed from outside.

The function of the new society is to make clear self-responsibility, to aid a person in becoming more self-aware, and to decide what rules society wants to make to postpone certain behaviors and to provide unaware colluders more time in which to become more aware.

If laws are to be made to reward awareness rather than unawareness, they should be changed gradually in order to give people an opportunity to understand the new perspective. Sick leave, for example, is a procedure that rewards unawareness since it sometimes rewards illness or dissembling with a vacation. It could be changed gradually by having days allowed for sick leave reduced and vacation days increased, say, at the rate of one day a year, to give people an opportunity to adjust. People are then rewarded for health rather than for illness.

## THE ONLY CRIME

There is only one crime: creating conditions that make options desired by others more difficult to attain. A crime is simply a continuation of unpleasant interaction, just as cancer is a continuation of chronic tension. If I create conditions you choose to find difficult, you will not like me, you will avoid me, you will combat me, you will try to talk me out of it, you will change how you react to my action, or you will try to stop me.

This definition of crime supports opposition to victimless crimes. Crimes against the self are nonsense. If people are self-responsible, it is only self-deceptive arrogance that leads governments to decide what is for a person's "own good." If I do not want to wear a seat belt or a crash helmet, that is my business. The state's business is to decide what it will do if I harm myself. If I get into a seat-beltless accident, and I ask the state to pay my medical bill, then the state has every right to refuse. If I risk injury, I am also responsible for the consequences of my risk. I might want to make a deal with the state. If it pays my medical bills, I will fasten my seat belt. That is perfectly legitimate, providing both parties agree. Any agreement between two people or groups that does not affect anyone else is legitimate. It is the same as any action by an individual that does not affect another.

John Stuart Mill expressed a similar feeling:

> The principle is, that the sole end for which mankind are warranted, individually, or collectively, in interfering with the liberty of action of any of their number is self-protection. That is, the only purpose for which power can be rightfully exercised over any member of a civilized community, against his will, is to prevent harm to others.
>
> His own good, either physical or moral, is not a sufficient warrant. He cannot rightfully be compelled to do or forbear because it will make him happier, because, in the opinion of others, to do so would be wise, or even right.
>
> These are good reasons for remonstrating with him, or persuading him, or entreating him, but not for compelling him, or visiting him with an evil in case he do otherwise. To justify that, the conduct from which it is desired to deter him must be calculated to produce evil to someone else.[67]

Whenever you are creating conditions that I choose to find limiting to me, the first place to deal with it is

between you and me. Most of the time we can resolve
our differences. If we do not, then an outside person
may be invited in. This person may be an official, like
a judge, or simply a person satisfactory to both of us,
one whom we both trust, like a counselor. The latter is
preferable to a judge. Decisions made among the people
affected by the decisions interfere with society the least
and encourage personal responsibility the most. If I
do not represent myself well, I will not get what I
want. Therefore, I am motivated to represent myself
well.

In an experiment in Tucson,[68] law officials tried
this approach. The victim of a certain crime (felonies)
and the criminal (first-time offenders) were brought
together with a facilitator. They exchanged versions of
what happened and negotiated the terms as to what
should be done. If they agreed, the case would not go
to court.

A young man stole a color television set. At their
meeting, he learned that his victim was an invalid old
woman, one for whom watching television was life's
central attraction. He understood that he had not just
stolen a TV, he had materially affected the quality
of the old woman's life. The outcome of their encounter
was that, in addition to returning her TV, he agreed
to paint her house, mow her lawn, and drive her to
the doctor for her weekly checkup. In another case,
the wealthy victim ultimately provided the offender
with a $10,000 scholarship to attend medical school.

After one year's operation, the program has been
successful in all but nine of the 204 cases which it
accepted (96 percent). The cost of resolution per case
was one-fifth of the cost for an average felony case
($304 to $1566).

This technique is simple, requires honesty and
greater awareness—the job of the facilitator—and
stresses that the responsibility for an action lies primarily with those who participate in the act, not with a
disinterested and often uninterested stranger—the
judge.

# LICENSING

Licensing has not proved an effective tool for
providing program quality assurance. More-
over, attempts by licensing to regulate or control program quality in general may do more
harm than good by creating barriers to developing needed services.
                    —Committee, California Assembly[69]

Lying is creating conditions within which I find it
difficult to function, that is, to choose a valuable option.
Just as my creating my own lie presents me with grave
difficulties, so your lying affects me similarly. Other
things do not fit, and I expend extra energy to reconcile them, just as eating food that is not compatible
with my body means that my body expends additional
energy to integrate body and food. Most of it must
be expelled; little is used. So it is with your life. A law
against dishonesty would render an important service
to the public and be a proper role for the law.
    Licensing of professionals has not been a notably
successful activity. Many licensed people are incompetent, and many unlicensed people are among the
most skilled. Several professional fields have blatantly
unclear criteria of excellence, and the establishment of
a board of professionals to decide what is not yet
scientifically decidable, such as psychotherapeutic success, invites political invasion. Licensing becomes a
vehicle for a special group to stake out an area and to
exclude outsiders from being economically competitive.
    Further, licensing is inconsistent with the principles
of truth and choice. Allowing a licensing procedure
to decide who can practice, and which consumers may
use the services of the practitioners, takes away the
right of choice from the consumer and does not
sufficiently emphasize the importance of honesty and

awareness in the professional-consumer relation—an
emphasis that may be enhanced by laws.

Recently, there have been attempts in some states
to introduce full disclosure as a substitute for licensing.
I will describe a version of such a full-disclosure law,
which is consistent with the principles of profound
simplicity.

All persons offering services aimed at enhancing the
human condition, either by relieving blockages, as in
psychotherapy, or by helping a consumer to realize
more of his or her potential through body work, mind,
psychological, educational, or spiritual activity, would
be required to provide potential consumers with a full
disclosure of all information relevant to the competence
of the professional. Such information would include
the practitioner's education, training, philosophy, fees,
membership in professional organizations, awards, and
anything else the professional feels is relevant. The
state agency charged with enforcing this law would
prepare a form for presenting this information and
would require it to be posted in the place of business
and to be available to each prospective customer. The
enforcing group would receive a copy of the practitioner's statement along with evidence supporting the statement, and would provide a symbol signifying the
veracity of the claims without evaluating them.

The role of the law is simply to determine lying,
not to usurp the choice of consumers. The law assumes
that role because, as a practical matter, it is too time
consuming for every potential customer to check every
assertion made by every potential professional.

Since the statements of qualification of the professional are all unequivocal—they know what their
education and training were—there are only two
reasons for inaccuracies: not being aware of the law
and deliberate lying. It is the obligation of the law-
maker to provide opportunities such that all professionals may be informed of the law. This may be
accomplished through publication of the law in public
media, special mailings to relevant groups, and the

provision of sufficient time, say, one year, for everyone to be informed. It is the choice of the professionals to be informed or not.

This accomplished, all violations are deliberate and premeditated. Since the purpose of the law is to prevent lying, the punishments are meant as deterrents and should be severe, say, one or possibly more years in jail.

Following incarceration, I still would not attempt to prevent a person from practicing. The former felon may continue to solicit customers as before. The only difference is that now the practitioner must include in full disclosure the fact of spending a year in jail for lying about qualifications.

There is no need for the state to decide the undecidable, namely, who is competent. There is no need for the state to determine unethical behavior, too often a thrust toward conformity. Whether a person was or was not trained at X institution in the year Y, whether that person got a degree at X in Y, whether a person passed certain examinations or has recommendations from certain people, are all decisions simple to determine accurately by a board.

In the present situation, I rely on the state to tell me who is competent, I passively submit myself to a professional, and if I do not like what he does, I sue for malpractice. My role is very inert and childlike. If I, as a consumer, know that I am responsible for selecting a counselor, I am likely to assume a more responsible stance. In many cases, the very act of being responsible will have a therapeutic effect.

Thus, choice and truth replace sham and image. Licensing does not protect the public. Licensing does not exclude incompetents. Licensing does not encourage innovation. It stultifies. Full disclosure treats both professional and consumer as responsible adults and alters the role of the law to one of determining truth, a function it can perform well in the service of its constituents.

## PRISON REFORM

The prison system has lately been the object of much investigation and of much criticism. Confusion over whether prisons are for rehabilitation or for punishment has led to demands for a restructuring of the system. The present approach suggests a few ideas for prison reform aimed at rehabilitation.

Self-responsibility is the key to rehabilitation and to the operation of a prison. As previously mentioned, the futility of trying to run an organization without the consent of the inmates is well known. To run a prison as an authoritarian structure certainly will not serve the end of teaching people to be self-responsible.

In 1840, when Alexander Maconochie became warden at Norfolk Island, Australia, he introduced a system where the inmates were given responsibility for helping to police themselves and for working their way out of prison through a point system. Of 1450 inmates released under the system, fewer than three percent were ever again convicted of a crime. Over a century later, in 1968, Thomas Murton, superintendent of the Arkansas State Penitentiary, proposed a partici-patory democracy system in which inmates would be given the responsibility of making important decisions concerning their lives, and risking real failure if they made the wrong ones. He set up an inmate council and a disciplinary committee elected by the inmates. Eventually, Murton planned to relinquish his veto power over the inmates' decisions, but he was fired before he had the opportunity.

Applications of the present approach are not identical with permissiveness. On the contrary, the concept of "helping," described above, requires that, to be most effective, prison officials must know when to be tough and when to be tender. A man who spent seventeen years in jail expressed this point well. Tom[70] sneered at efforts made to rehabilitate him. His immigrant father would not make a living, and his mother was in and out of mental hospitals. Social workers did nothing but say: "Poor baby, did you have it that bad?" All that did, he said, was reinforce his weaknesses.

He joined Delancey Street, an organization, in this respect, run along lines similar to the profound simplicity principles.[71] Over and over, he was told that he was "an asshole" and that it was about time he did something to change himself. That did it for him. Feeling sorry for criminals and excusing their behavior because of their backgrounds is not the answer, he is convinced. "We should be putting the responsibility on the individual. Society should be kicking our behinds when we need it, and then saying: 'We are going to provide you with marketable skills and help you get a job if you want it. And if you don't, the hell with you.' "

This is an eloquent statement that society would do best to choose to help criminals realize that they are choosing their own lives and to make it easier for them to choose adaptive lives. If they do not respond to this approach, society takes the view that they are choosing to be dependent on society, and it can do what it pleases with them. Removing them from society is one path.

The concept of a prison, that is, one location where all prisoners are kept, is another very questionable one.

When musicians go to Aspen in the summer, their musical side emerges. Reams of people share their interest in piano or composition. The shared aspects of their life are reinforced.

When criminals are placed in a prison, they talk and think a great deal about crime. They discuss criminal life, crime strategies, how to beat the law. They too are immersed in the things they have in common with their sub-society.

Television operates like a giant society. Anything on the screen, especially new, must be what everyone is doing. If I had not seen TV dramas, movies, and plays about crime, I doubt that I would have had any appreciable experience with crime in my entire life. The varieties of crime and the various ways to perform it would barely have entered my thinking. I would have been preoccupied with my own life and experience.

ABC once presented a two-hour special on the Olympic Games. Since 1896, the modern Olympics have been the arena for some of humankind's greatest moments, moments of great achievements of the human body, mind, and spirit. New potentials were realized in speed, strength, grace, agility, flexibility, stamina, and courage. Yet a full one-fourth of the ABC program was devoted to political wrangles; another one-fourth to the terrorists of 1972. Their message speaks loudly: Tragedy is more important, that is, newsworthy, than realized potential. Pity.

The appearance of an event in the media implies that it is important. People who have inclusion problems, that is, people who have problems knowing what is important, are given a set of guidelines by the media. Murders are important. So are wars, hijackings, fires, plane crashes, terrorists, kidnappings, strikes, and assassinations. Not important is an encounter group in which two people have a rebirth and whose lives are forever changed for the better; not important is a couple who learns to live happily with each other; not important is a man who discovers his body—how to move it and how to get more pleasure from it. If I want to be "in," if I want to participate in sparkling cocktail talk, I interest myself in TV's headline events.

What should be done so that these phenomena would emphasize more profitable aspects of life? Fill the media with options, especially those options which seem more conducive to growth. Develop programs for criminals that involve including them with noncriminals. Place hospital patients, both mental and physical, in community settings, or at least interplace them among themselves so that they are exposed to alternative ways of coping with life.

In this way, aspects of inmates other than the criminal ones would be supported. Just as assuming

and supporting participant self-responsibility in encounter groups brings out participant strength, so would
assuming and supporting noncriminal traits in criminals elicit the strong parts of the criminals' personalities.

Prison reform then includes creating conditions in
which prisoners would find it easier to develop their
noncriminal sides. And it includes creating circumstances to ease a transition to that state.

# MEDICINE

> It is the body that is the hero, not science, not
> antibiotics . . . not machines or new devices.
> . . . The task of the physician today is what it
> always has been, to help the body do what it
> has learned so well to do on its own during its
> unending struggle for survival—to heal itself.
> It is the body, not medicine, that is the hero.
> —R. Glasser, M.D.[72]

If medicine followed the principles of profound simplicity, its new banner would read: "Patient, heal thyself."

The medical model is based on the assumption that the expert, the physician, knows about illness and that the patient does not. The physician, therefore, is responsible for the patient, meaning that the physician has the power in the relationship. The medical model also assumes that disease is unrelated to the diseased. Disease follows certain laws, like germ theory, cholesterol accumulation, or blood pressure buildup. Physicians know about these matters, it is assumed, and lay persons do not.

The absurdity of these assumptions leads to a distorted approach to disease. The medical approach assumes that I, the patient, walk blithely through life almost totally unrelated to my health, my illnesses, or my injuries. Ill health occurs because I am the "victim" of foreign bodies such as viruses, bacteria, and germs that come in epidemics. Whether I become ill is at the whim or the capriciousness of nature. Pure chance places viruses and bacteria in the air I breathe, the food I eat, the water I drink. Perhaps a touch of responsibility is given me if I fail to follow the doctor's orders or wear my galoshes, if I sit in a draft or work too hard. Even these personal contributions become puny, however, when it is noted how many healthy people disobey doctors' orders, never wear galoshes, and sit in freezing drafts working too hard.

After contracting a disease through no fault of my own, I get rid of the disease also through outside agents unrelated to myself. I go to a doctor who tells me what is wrong and what drug I should ingest or which operation I should have in order to rid myself of the ailment. If I get well, it is because I have a good doctor and the drug or the operation is effective. My only contribution is to be an obedient follower of the doctor's orders. Or, perhaps, through a genetic "accident," I have a healthy constitution which may contribute to my recovery.

If this fiction of the inert patient were abandoned, all medicine would be altered. Here is the opposite scenario.

I am responsible for contracting illnesses and I am the one who heals myself. Viruses and the like are constantly present inside and outside my body. They are not my enemies. They are not in themselves poisonous. On the contrary, they are part of the balance of nature and have a definite, positive role to play. They take on the nature of their environment. If bacteria exist in a healthy body, they are helpful in aiding an existing function as, for example, aiding the digestive process. If they are in a toxic environment, they become toxic and enhance the toxic process. Pasteur's purported deathbed declaration in 1895 reflected his realization of this: "Bernard was right. The microbe is nothing, the terrain is everything."[73]

If, at some level of my awareness, I decide to become ill, I will weaken my body and fail to eliminate poisons, thereby creating a toxic environment for viruses. I stop the functioning of the immune system, allow an invasion of foreign entities, and become ill.[72] The decision about illness has been made throughout my life as my organism developed. If I decided early to be healthy, I developed my organism to withstand any condition that would lead to illness. If I found illness functional, either chronically or occasionally, I developed my body appropriately. I do not always let myself know that I am choosing to be ill. I am not always aware or conscious that I am choosing. Some situations require more resistance than others, and I sometimes have not let myself know how to resist a given situation.

I also heal myself. Within my body is the knowledge and ability for self-healing. All I need to do is to choose at the appropriate level of awareness, to be well, and to learn about my bodymind. Given rest and my un-conflicted desire for health, my body will repair any damage that it has sustained. If the damage is very extensive, and reasons for it are very deep inside me, then I must discover why I decided to be ill, how I am now benefiting from it, and how to change it. This may be done with the aid of many of the human potential methods.[7]

Through bodymind work I heal myself. Externally imposed drugs simply suppress symptoms, they do not heal. Aspirin relieves the "pain" of a headache, peni-cillin reduces the "symptoms" of pneumonia. However, the toxic condition that led to the disease remains, and, in addition, the drug I have taken must be dealt with by my body.

If this view of disease is accepted—the view that I am responsible for contracting a disease and that I am responsible for healing myself—then the emphasis of the physician would be to create conditions within which I would choose to become aware of the true nature of disease, to see that I have chosen to be sick, and to become aware of whether I want to become well. If I want to become well, I may wish the physician to introduce me to techniques for discovering the origin of the illness and for healing myself. When the healing is done this way, the cause of the disease is actually eliminated. It is more than the suppression of symptoms.

Probably the most dramatic illustration of the practical application of this viewpoint in medicine lies in the work of the Simontons.[4] Starting with 110 stage IV cancer patients—those declared terminal or "incurable" by physicians—with metastatic cancer (that is, cancers in more than one location), and who were projected to have no more than six to twelve months to live, the Simontons subjected them to a complete regimen. Patients had regular group therapy in which responsibility for contracting and continuing the cancer was explored. They continued radiation and chemotherapy treatments although some patients voluntarily terminated these after a while. Patients did a short guided fantasy in which they first visualized the cancer cells, then visualized the white blood cells destroying the cancer cells, and then visualized the healthy tissue after the battle. They usually did this fantasy twice a day.

After two years, 81 percent of their patients are still alive. Forty percent are in remission or are completely free of cancer symptoms, and 35 percent have completely arrested symptoms.

These remarkable results are based on patients taking responsibility for their own cures. The role of the doctor is to help the patients understand how and why they brought about their illnesses and to provide them with a technique for dealing with themselves. The philosophy also assumes that cancer is a disease of the total organism—body, mind, and spirit—and that it is to be understood as a part of an ongoing life style rather than as a specific virus accidentally contracted from eating or breathing a carcinogenic agent.

The places where allopathic medicine—that practiced in the Western world—may be of assistance are in testing the state of the organism, in some surgical procedures where body functioning is obstructed, and in prolonging life until patients can take over their own healing, that is, until they choose to be more aware. These last two functions fulfill the principle of transition.

Malpractice suits will diminish as soon as both physicians and patients accept the fact that physicians are not responsible for any patient and do not cure anyone. The physician chooses to help me, the patient, understand that I am choosing my illness, and to present me with options I did not let myself know existed. Physicians are not responsible for me. I am responsible for myself. What physicians can do is to simplify the process of patient self-responsibility and patient healing as would any good teacher. Teachers do not get sued for malpractice because they do not make hubristic claims that they are responsible for a student's learning. Malpractice woes are what doctors ask for by concocting, along with patients, the grandiose fairy tale that they cure patients.

That I am responsible for my health and my illness is not a moralistic statement. It does not say that my health is my fault, or that I am to blame, or that I have been careless, wrong, bad, or immoral. It simply says that I choose. It is a statement of what is, not an evaluation or a judgment.

If I want to look at what I have done as bad, I can choose to do that too. That is simply another choice. I am choosing to evaluate what I have chosen as bad, perhaps because I get some pleasure from anguishing or from feeling depressed.

Your role as doctor is likewise unevaluative. Your job is to aid me in finding out what is. You may also, as a person, have some feeling about what I choose to do about my health, but that is all it is. You are saying: "I want you to make choices other than those you have been making for yourself." I am free to deal with your desires in whatever way I choose.

This conception returns the word "doctor" to its original meaning, derived from the Latin docere, to teach. The doctor creates conditions that are conducive to patients learning about themselves, particularly about their own organisms.

The issue of whether people should be kept alive by artificial means, as in the famous case of Karen Quinlan, takes on a different look from this perspective. The debate in the Quinlan case was over whether the parents had the right to take her off the mechanical devices that were presumably prolonging her life and let her die "with dignity," an odd phrase. The argument was between the parents and the doctors. No one wondered about Karen's desires, because she was assumed to be incapable of choosing.

In fact, Karen Quinlan is deciding for herself whether she wants to die. Many people on life-preserving machines have expired. Many people taken off the machines have lived. At the appropriate level of their organisms, they are choosing.

Whether a doctor wants to continue instruments, or whether a parent wants a child taken off instruments, is decided in terms of the doctor's or the parents' wishes, not the patient's. Perhaps the parents are tired of the expense and energy involved, or perhaps the doctor does not want to give up, all perfectly human reasons. But letting someone "die with dignity" or for other ostensibly altruistic reasons muddies the waters with self-deception.

Intriguing and predictable from this viewpoint, the epilogue to this case is that Karen Quinlan was taken off the machines and, to everyone's amazement, did not die. At this writing, she has been alive for over two years after being taken off the machines.

Doctors act like doctors because patients collude with them. Many patients have a desire to give up responsibility for their health to someone else and then to hold that person responsible if they are not well. If so many patients did not like the role of helpless invalid, doctors would not occupy the position they now have.

This situation parallels the one described above under licensing, where the consumer takes a childlike role. As a medical patient, typically, I assume that I do not know anything about my illness. Nor do I know whom to go to for assistance unless I am told by others, in this case the board which licenses physicians. I then take an inert role, and if the physician's work does not please me, I will sue him or her.

Ultimately, illness is a learning experience. By taking responsibility for my illness, I, the patient, have an opportunity to learn more about myself through finding out why I chose to be ill in that particular way at that particular time. Life-changing experiences may occur at illness times if the patient is willing to take this perspective.

Beth came into my encounter group about one month after she had been diagnosed as having leukemia. For the first four days of the five-day workshop, she looked morose and did not say a word. Finally, after several people had expressed interest in her, Beth agreed to say how she was feeling. She sat in the center of the group, became very anxious, and pulled her long hair over her face. After a few moments, she went over and faced the wall, her back to the group. A long pause preceded her first words. "I am a terrible person." She proceeded to tell us how she caused her husband to commit suicide, had virtually abandoned her children, had caused her parents untold agony and misery, and had been a great burden to her friends.

After hearing Beth's macabre tale of her dark side, and after she had expressed it all while many group members were supporting her, the group gave Beth its reaction: Bullshit!

Clearly, this was not what she had anticipated, and she was startled enough to even clear away a sliver of her hair so she could take a small peek at the group. "Who do you think you are, Beth, that you have the power to destroy people or to ruin their lives? You sound like God."

She began to see that responsibility for suicides is with the suicide, and that parents can choose to be hurt and devastated by their children if that is the kind of parents they choose to be. Soon Beth started to lighten visibly and began to reflect. The idea that the leukemia might be a self-punishment for her dolorous deeds began to dawn on her, and the absurdity of the situation struck her.

The next day, Beth returned bright and fresh with some jokes. She turned out to be very witty, her specialty being "cleans and dirties" (her best: Warrior is clean; gladiator is dirty). She started jogging with some group members and within two weeks jogged nine miles in one day. At her next physical examination two months later, her doctor would not believe the results. She was totally free of symptoms and still is today, two years later. Not only is Beth's illness cleared up, but she was able to use the experience of illness to understand and improve her life, the ultimate function of disease.

# POLITICS

The goal of democracy is to continually reduce
the need for governmental or administrative
interference and to steadily increase the power
of self-management of social groupings by
constantly removing the obstacles in the way
of self-regulation . . . To secure the peace
and freedom and the facilities to get at the
"obstacles in the way" is therefore the basic
task of all research and social organization,
be it in the combat of poverty, or desert, or in
the overcoming of gravity.

—Wilhelm Reich[74]

Out of the backwash of initial excitement of the
human potential movement emerged the issue of individual versus group, inner revolution versus outer
revolution, personal growth versus social action. The
formulation in some of the more righteous exegeses[75]
is narcissism versus selflessness.

During the late 1960s and early 1970s when the
human potential and the social activism movements
were thriving, there were many clashes on this issue.
I once met with one of the pioneers of the Berkeley
Free Speech Movement, Mike Rossman, in mortal
verbal combat to decide whose way of changing the
world was "right." Other than becoming personally
closer, the debate did not seem to dislodge either of us
from our secret hold on the truth.

From the activist's point of view, the primary problem was that encounter was an opiate of the people.
If we helped people resolve their personal problems,

their motivation for righting social injustice would wane. I felt that social action without self-awareness leads to terrorist-type self-destruction, which helps to destroy the very cause espoused.

The social work-religious orientation presents the issue in terms of being my brother's (now sibling's) keeper. "It is not ethical to abandon responsibility for one's fellows if we are to remain a viable biological species and if we are to retain the trappings of human-ness." This concern rose as the human potential movement of the mid-seventies, prompted by Erhard (est), Greenwald, Seth, myself, and the memory of Fritz Perls, veered more and more toward a radical view of self-responsibility and choice. "I am responsi-ble for myself and for no one else unless I choose to be." This solidification of view joined the issue more clearly.

As one who adheres to the strong self-choice view, I would like to present the case for "narcissism" being the most desirable stance interpersonally and for lead-ing to the most satisfactory society.

It is customary to equate such terms as help, com-passion, empathy, and caring with social responsibility and in opposition to personal choice. I feel that quite the opposite is true.

Jane, obviously very disturbed, extremely frightened, and highly sensitive, came to a recent group I was co-leading with Valerie. Her fear was so great that Jane took to bringing a blanket to each meeting. She cried easily. She looked dark, saggy, and awful. She was constantly ill. Her tale was heartrending. She had certainly been miserable; life had dealt her a bad hand and she was trying gamely to survive. Several people in the group were very "helpful." They sympathized, provided Kleenex, sat next to her, supported her, stayed up with her all night, reinforced her feelings with parallel stories of their own, brought her meals to her, praised her efforts at overcoming her sorrows, and gave her considerable physical support.

Strangely, this caring, helpful, empathetic behavior,

which it sincerely was, was of little help. Jane continued to look moribund and sought out Valerie and then me to talk to privately, feeling that her problems were much too deep and her condition far too precarious to risk with a group of amateurs. We declined her request and urged her to work in the group.

Finally, Valerie, who is much more spontaneous than I am, could stand it no longer. At one meeting, she exploded at Jane. "You are the sorriest bitch I have ever seen! You've been playing the tragedy queen all week, and you've played it in the last six groups you've been in. You're asking everyone to feel sorry for you while you're probably the gutsiest lady here," Valerie roared across the room, warming to her task. She grabbed Jane's blanket, and Jane, supposedly so weak, held on as Valerie dragged both blanket and body into the center of the room. The group sat stunned. Jane was furious beneath her display of hurt and oppressedness.

Then Jane and Valerie began to wrestle. Valerie, a half foot shorter and considerably lighter, won easily. Jane lay on the floor looking martyred. Valerie threw the blanket in her face then said the magic words: "It's bad enough that you go around spewing out this poor, fucked-over act, but you could at least be entertaining. You aren't even the best tragedy queen in this workshop. Nancy, over in Dave's group, does it much better than you do. You should go over and get some pointers from her so that at least you'd be convincing. Your act is boring."

With that Jane raised her head and out came that familiar telltale look that occurs when someone knows his or her game has been laid bare. A sly smile crept over her face. The group broke out in great, tension-releasing laughter. Jane grabbed Valerie with a combination of anger and warmth, and they hugged.

I moved in and we explored why Jane was choosing to be miserable. She was now at a place to hear the possibility that she was not one of God's chosen victims, but that she had chosen to interpret her life as sorrowful and miserable. We explored where this choice came from and what value she was deriving from living this way, right now.

As soon as the floodgates were down, Jane went right to the truth. During Jane's exploration, Valerie's physical place right near her, supporting her, touching her, was really helpful. It was not a collusion to allow Jane to continue her game-playing. It was support to help her let herself become aware of motives she had been hiding from herself.

To continue her breakthrough beyond the verbal, I asked Jane if she would be willing to burn her blanket. There followed a long period of anguishing and conflict. The laughter had died, the verbal breakthrough had been made, but would she be willing to give up what she now knew was false security? While she fretted, I asked her to tell us the truth behind her game of "poor, miserable Jane." She proceeded to tell us of her remarkable talents and accomplishments, a truly imposing list. As she finished, she looked at the group, paused a long time, and said: "Let's go burn the blanket."

We all went outside and held a marvelous blanket-burning ritual. Jane had to work hard to burn the blanket. It was damp and drizzling outside, and the blanket was made of wool from which the lanolin had not been removed. Burning it took nearly an hour of exhausting effort and a multitude of newspapers. Jane even waved her coat at the fire to make more flame. When it was done, Jane, who had been walking around like an invalid all week, was rosy-cheeked, vigorous, and hungry. And she and the rest of us felt very good.

At the next meeting, someone else started talking like a victim. To our delight, Jane came sailing in to take over. She started pointing out the game of victim. The patient became the therapist, the student became the teacher, one of the surest ways to deepen learning. Jane, three years later, is functioning very effectively and regards Valerie as a valued friend.

This is the point: Helping is a fine art. It is far more

than support. The indiscriminate use of sympathy,
Kleenex, and hugs is an attempt to establish the sup-
porter as a wonderful person. Whether it really is what
the supported person needs is almost irrelevant. Valerie
was truly helpful because she took the time to listen,
to see through the bullshit, to refuse to collude in
Jane's misery, to be willing to risk the opprobrium of
the group, and to risk being just plain wrong.

She also had to be aware that Jane was choosing
to be miserable. If she had agreed with the prevailing
belief, that poor Jane's troubles were the result of an
impoverished household, divorced parents, weak father,
alcoholic husband, sickly constitution, and so on,
then it never would have occurred to Valerie to do what
she did. Valerie realized that Jane did it to herself
and, therefore, could stop doing it to herself.

This is the liberal paradox. Having the "oppressed"
take responsibility for their oppression sounds illiberal,
but this position returns the power to the oppressed.
As long as Jane let herself believe that her tragic condition was the fault of vicious earthly forces, she
paralyzed herself from doing anything productive.
When she finally accepted this illiberal dogma, her eyes
lit up, she lightened, brightened, and sparkled. She
had been living with a lie, the lie that she was not
responsible for herself. That lie required many subsequent events to be distorted to be consistent with
the lie.

What Jane realized was that all the events of her
life were indeed real; that if she wanted to, she could
see them as tragic; that if she wanted to, she could
see herself as having no responsibility for them; that
if she wanted to, she could blame her lackluster personal functioning on these events; and that if she
wanted to, she could feel angry and miserable. What
the experience did for her was to help her see all the
"if she wanted to" portions of the above statement.
She was deciding her life. She could change it. When
she saw that, she could help herself. And she did.

What Valerie was doing was deciding to create conditions that might help Jane become more aware of her self-deceptions—and perhaps to choose to change. Valerie did it because she liked Jane, because she likes to feel like a competent group leader, because she likes to think of herself as a good person. She also did it because she herself has played the victim game and enjoys seeing someone else break the game she broke. I could say that she did it for Jane, but that is not true. If the above reasons did not exist, Valerie probably would not have done it at all.

If Valerie felt that Jane would profit from support, as she did when Jane started to let herself know about her own self-choice, then Valerie gave support. Support at that point was helpful. It is not the specific action that is helpful; it is the timing and appropriateness of the action. In that sense, helping is a fine art.

Helping skill depends not only on understanding self-choice, but also on the helper's self-awareness. Unfortunately, many socially conscious people use social events to work out their own problems. As a consequence, they are often indignant with those who are not socially active, and their own work is of limited value.

During the height of the black turmoil in the late 1960s, I was asked to go to Seaside, California, to help the blacks there. My colleagues and I drove fifty miles from our homes in Big Sur to attend one of their night meetings. After polite introductions, one ghetto black looked at us and said: "What are you doing here? Why did you leave your warm fireplaces and drive fifty miles in the rain? How can you care about us? You don't even know us."

I sputtered, then launched into a glib statement about social justice, brotherhood, the skills we have that could be useful, and, er, uh . . . He just stared at me. What *was* I doing here? I *was* reluctant to leave my house. We were late. I did not know them. I might not even like them. Why was I here?

He moved into the space created by my pause. "Look. You're white. If you went to our streets, it would take you two years to get anyone to trust you. You're no good to us." I resisted hearing him. I had never thought of that. Then what he was getting at hit me.

I did know why I was there. I wanted everyone to know that I was a socially conscious liberal who donated his time for worthy causes. In short, I wanted people to know that I was wonderful. When I finally acknowledged that, I could accept that I did not really want to be there, that it was unlikely that I could be helpful, that a better thing to do might be to train black people to go into their own streets, and that perhaps I should just wait until the big black-white charge subsided and then see what I wanted to do.

We soon left, never to return. The Seaside blacks worked out their own program. They had helped us to be self-aware social actors. The outcome of our self-awareness could have been to lobby for legislation, to educate whites, perhaps to strike or to revolt. No action is prohibited because social actors are self-aware. The main consequence of our awareness is that whatever social action we decide to undertake had a much better chance of actually being effective.

## WELFARE

It is neither necessary nor helpful to proclaim one's wonderfulness and selflessness toward others. It is probably a lie anyway and is not needed for a successful society. If I act in ways people do not like, more than likely I will elicit consequences I do not want. If I feel I am a person I do not like, I will not be happy. That is enough. That is sufficient to motivate me to change the way I behave so that I will like myself better. These motivations, for me and for everyone, are sufficient to lead to the ideal society.

In his typically insightful, trenchant way, Robert Benchley once wrote an essay on looking at group pictures. While others were around, he would ooh and aah and admire the baby. He would say how young Grandma looked. Then when the others were gone, he would go through all the pictures and spend hours examining himself. If you ask people what happened at their last group meeting, they will inevitably tell you what happened to them. Whenever I see a new book on humanistic or social psychology, I wait until no one is looking, then I turn to the index and read all the references to me. People see the world in terms of themselves.

And that is all right. Unfortunately, what some critics become entrapped by is the failure to discriminate between what is and how they evaluate what is.

What is, is that we are each organized around ourselves. Even Schweitzers must feel gratified by sacrificing or they would not do it. The real difference is that some people are gratified by actions other people find helpful, and others are gratified, at least temporarily, by actions other people find difficult to deal with. Members of society would benefit from starting from the premise of self-responsibility, avoiding the hypocrisy of "self-sacrifice," and dealing with each other in terms of the way things really are.

A famous Talmudic story points to a simple pervasive principle for social action. If you meet a hungry man and give him a fish, he will not be hungry, but, if you teach him to fish, he will never be hungry. (I would now change that to: if you create conditions within which he chooses to learn to fish . . .)

Our current federal welfare program is a fish-giving procedure. To provide poor people with welfare, as we do now, is to give them, for an indefinite time, barely enough money to exist. This treats them as children being given an allowance and makes it difficult for them to become self-supporting. A totally different message is communicated if welfare were recognized as an instrument to help recipients understand that they are choosing their condition and that they could choose not to be indigent, and that the state is willing to help them while they make the transition from dependent to independent. This stance conveys a message of confidence in the welfare recipient's inner resources.

The welfare mechanism suggested by this policy is to give each welfare recipient more money than is presently given, and for a shorter period of time. Welfare recipients would be given enough money to live reasonably well and to have the time and resources for schooling or training of some kind. The money would stop at a designated time, after, say, three years. By that time, the state assumes the person would become independent.

After this point, the recipient would receive no more welfare money. In this way, the government avoids being moralistic or magnanimous, and the welfare recipient is spared the role of infant. The government takes responsibility for itself, choosing to be temporarily supportive, following the principle of transition, then choosing to refuse support to a person who has not become independent. Likewise, the recipient's choice is clear: Become self-sufficient, with aid, or receive no more welfare money and be poverty-stricken.

If this proves unreasonably harsh, the program would be adjusted appropriately. Perhaps the time period of support should be longer, the money greater, and perhaps counseling should be provided or special schools set up. A hearing procedure could be set up in special cases, as in the case of a person who has almost completed school or a single parent who is still involved in the bonding process with a child. These are issues which may be met as they arise.

This model for a poverty program is not unprecedented within the federal government. One of the most successful pieces of social legislation ever enacted was the G.I. Bill passed after World War II.

In the educational area, the G.I. Bill was a model for the principles of choice and transition. Qualified veterans were provided with enough money for their education, books, materials, and expenses—and were provided this assistance for a limited time—until they completed their education or, more specifically, as long as they were progressing successfully toward an educational goal.

When they completed that goal, the government stopped paying—forever. The message from the government was this: We feel you are capable of completing training that will assist you to become a self-reliant citizen. We choose to support you, generously, for a reasonable time. This is temporary support aimed at easing your transition to independence. We do not intend to support you beyond that point, because we assume you are capable of self-support.

The success of the G.I. Bill is legendary. It is largely responsible for the great postwar boom in skilled personnel. To participate in it was in no way demeaning. Recipients were not objects of opprobrium as is often true of those now receiving welfare. The money was spent with great efficiency. The country probably received many times what it invested as tens of thousands of people, who probably never would have without the G.I. Bill, received advanced training.

This new policy requires trusting people. If people let themselves be aware, they can run their lives the way they want to. We truly help each other by creating conditions under which we find it easy to take responsibility for ourselves. This means finding and telling the truth. It means being aware.

## TAXATION

Taxes are far too complicated. Billions are spent in the preparation and collection of taxes. The principle of simplicity is violated. The basis for taxation seems to miss the point.

Taxes are the contribution of each person to projects that are too large for individuals to carry out efficiently, and which are of benefit for all, or nearly all. They are not necessary when each person provides for himself or for herself. The purpose of taxes is to provide for public institutions such as schools and highways, to support private enterprise through tax benefits and subsidies, to provide for the welfare of those in need, as in health and welfare, and to provide national security.

I should pay taxes to the degree that I enjoy the benefits of the tax expenditures. Taxing the amount of money I acquire, that is, income tax, is irrelevant. No matter how much money I have acquired, I do not enjoy the benefits of taxation unless I spend my money. I cannot enjoy the highways unless I have a car. All I have is piles of paper if I do not buy anything. It is the acquisition and use of tax-produced benefits that should be taxed. The more I profit from the quality of life abetted by tax expenditures, the more I should contribute.

This leads to a specific proposal: Eliminate all but the sales tax. Let the sales tax be sharply graduated, depending upon the necessity of the object purchased. If something is a virtual necessity, such as basic food, the tax would be virtually zero. If something is a luxury, such as a yacht, the tax would be huge. In between, tax rates would vary appropriately. This would be the only tax we would have.

The message to the citizen is this: Make your money any way you wish, any way that is legal, and pay no tax. Pay only when you benefit from your income. If you live lavishly, you contribute lavishly. If you do not take much from the society, you do not pay much.

A tax board would be set up to determine: (1) the relative percentage of tax on each item or service; (2) the absolute amount; (3) the method of tax collection; and (4) the allocation of taxes collected. Several first approximations may be employed:

1. For taxation rates, begin by taxing an item inversely to the number sold or used, assuming that there is a greater demand for necessities than for luxuries. The number of loaves of bread sold is certainly greater than the number of Ferraris. There will be exceptions, but this would be a good place to start, probably accurate for a large proportion of items.

2. The absolute amount of each tax is calculated by determining the total amount of tax money needed by the country, estimating the total amount of taxable goods and services, and setting the rate so that the total taxes will equal the national requirement.

3. Collection would be computerized as much as possible. Retail stores could ring up sales so that amount and allocation of taxes would be recorded automatically. Where feasible, the system of credit cards connected with banks or tax collection centers would be used whereby sales would be automatically deducted from the bank account of the purchaser and added to the account of the store and of the government recipients. Such a system is now being tested. Collection would become a miniscule problem compared with the problem it presents to the present system.

4. The first approximation for allocating taxes collected would be to divide them equally among the federal, state, county, and local governments, giving the most tax money to the places where there are the most people. Everyone is thereby provided with the same opportunity to profit from tax expenditures.

Clearly, the tax board would have several problems, such as taxes on foreign spending, bartering, and the treatment of gifts, but they seem straightforward and amenable to reason, experience, and the constant changes bound to occur as the system shakes down.

The advantages are many: (1) Inequities in tax laws would virtually disappear. (2) Cost of computing and collecting taxes would be reduced by millions. (3) Cheating would be made extremely difficult. Since cheating would be primarily planned and deliberate, as with licensing, strong penalties would probably be effective deterrents. Something like a mandatory twenty-year jail term, without parole, for cheating would be appropriate. (4) The tax burden would be fairly divided. No longer would millionaires pay nothing. The system rewards only hoarding, and there is very little advantage to that. (5) Taxes would be collected constantly so that the government would have a better idea of its fiscal condition at any moment, and taxpayers would not have to endure the trauma of an annual taxpaying time. (6) The cost of creating new laws and of administering and integrating the present tax laws would be enormously reduced.

To make a tax law consistent with self-responsibility, all inheritance would be eliminated. All of a person's assets at death would be given to the government and divided just as tax money is divided. If I want to give something to you, I would have to do it in my lifetime.

The incentive in such a society is to make no more money than I can use and to enjoy my money while I live. If I enjoy philanthropy, of course, I can give money or goods or services away. But the incentive for accumulating and saving large fortunes would be eliminated.

In this system the major purposes of the law are to equate contributions to the society, to encourage personal enjoyment, and to prevent dishonesty.

When an $800,000-a-year corporation executive is fined $1,000 for falsely reporting a political campaign contribution, this is a joke. It is clear that such a law is not serious about preventing lies. Lying, probably more than any other single cause, prevents efficient government and probably can be effectively limited by severe deterrents. If a company were caught lying about taxes, it might be fined the gross income of the company for one year plus ten-year jail sentences for all personnel involved. In other words, the penalty for lying would be to eliminate the corporation as run by the culprits. In this case, the legal message is clear: Do not lie. If you do, we will choose to seriously dampen your career. My guess is that under those conditions, dishonesty would atrophy.

# SPORTS

Everything starts with yourself—with you making up your mind about what you're going to do with your life. I tell kids that it's a cruel world, and that the world will bend them either left or right, and it's up to them to decide which way to bend.
—Tony Dorsett, football player[76]

Sports is the Western yoga. Using our bodies for socially acceptable purposes occurs primarily in sports and in dance. The present approach has many applications to sports, some of which would be revolutionary, some merely clarifying of certain already existing trends.

Recognition of interpersonal factors is one of the latter. The effect of the relations among the players on their productivity has become clearer in recent years. The team concept in professional basketball of the Golden State Warriors of 1975-1976 and the Portland Trailblazers of 1977-1978 has been widely admired and emulated. The coaches of these teams managed to use all the players on the team so that they were mutually supportive and dedicated to playing their best. Stardom on the team was quite changeable which was apparently acceptable to all. Using this approach, the Warriors produced one of the most spectacular upsets in basketball history by winning the championship, defeating a heavily favored Washington team four games to zero.

Interpersonal factors are acknowledged informally on

sports teams quite often. "Troublemakers" are traded away; managers who do not "communicate" with their players are fired; one baseball catcher pairs best with a particular pitcher; all-star teams are often not as successful as teams with less skillful players.

Direct use of encounter techniques may deal with these issues more directly, resolve them, and lead to more effective play and personal growth on the part of the individuals involved.

## COMPETITION

Competition is a hotly debated topic. Feelings about competition range from the extreme advocacy of the ruthlessly competitive, such as Vince Lombardi, whose "Winning isn't everything, it's the only thing" is now cliché, to the extreme disavowal (or purported disavowal) of competition symbolized by the "New Games"[77] philosophy.

Competition is deleterious when it leads me to cheating, to excessive energy output devoted to winning (so that it leads to loss of feeling of myself), or to putting down my opponent. Competition is valuable when it leads me to develop a part of my potential that would be extremely difficult for me to develop alone. In that sense, my opponent gives me a gift. This is, perhaps, the most valuable way of looking at competition.

If I practice tennis all day by hitting the ball against a wall, it is unlikely that I will exercise my ability to play tennis nearly so well as if I play three sets of tennis with a player near my ability. His presence requires me to call upon speed, coordination, strength, and thinking not required by sparring with a wall. In that sense, he gives me a gift. Most people recognize this element by the fact that they continually seek partners, even if they lose.

Occasionally, competition is transcended. The game takes on a quality beyond the winning or losing. The experience is very much like a mystical experience. The thrill of the game, the atmosphere, the drama, the struggle, the supreme achievements of the contestants, transform the experience into a spiritual one: the 1976 Winter Olympics with Dorothy Hamill; Olga Korbut in the 1972 Olympics; the third Ali-Frazier fight when both acknowledged each other's greatness; the sixth game of the Phoenix-Golden State basketball playoff of 1976.

Competition is usually transcended by those who allow themselves to experience fully all of the feelings involved in the competitive situation. The principle of completion indicates that when I avoid feelings of competitiveness, especially by denying them, I must constantly expend energy keeping these feelings out of awareness. Experiencing the feelings allows me to go through them and to experience what comes next.

Pete Rose, the ex-Cincinnati third baseman, illustrated this phenomenon in the classic 1975 World Series. Rose is known as, perhaps, baseball's most competitive player. His nickname is Charlie Hustle. After a brilliant sixth game, Rose turned to Carlton Fisk of the opposing Boston Red Sox and exulted in the current athlete's cliché, "This is some kinduva game." Rose was exuberant. And his team had lost!

Here was Pete Rose, one of baseball's fiercest competitors, ecstatic after losing. He had apparently transcended win-lose and was fully appreciating the esthetic, perhaps mystical, beauty of a game brilliantly played. It was not accidental that it was Pete Rose who sensed this. He had allowed himself to be as fully competitive as he felt, so he could evolve beyond competition.

There is often a reluctance by an athlete to acknowledge this transcendent experience.[78] In fact, these events are often suppressed because they are not rewarded. If we could bring them to light and feature them as transcendent human experiences, sports would be broadened into a more total human activity.

## REFEREES

A great source of trouble in sport as well as in law is the premature use of referees and judges. The problem is universal, and there is no better place to illustrate it than in sports. Recently, I wrote an impassioned letter on the subject as it applies to the wonderful game of handball:[79]

After listening to lectures from the handball experts about ingenious strategies, new shots, amazing executions, marvelous conditioning and other wonders of this game, suddenly a sour note. I hear of how some players try to cheat, "finesse" was the euphemism, with hinders, double bounces, time outs, and so on. Cheating in a game like this! Who needs it? Mastery of the game is an intellectual, physical, and esthetic achievement. To sully it with cheating seems blasphemous.

It seems to me that handball—the perfect game —has an opportunity to model for other sports, indeed, to model for human life, a mode of human relating. Handball has the opportunity to present to the public not only a new sport, but also a new ethic.

Most sports have become arenas for how-to-cheat-and-not-get-caught. Many football and basketball coaches actually train their players in such techniques. This approach is not basically different from Watergate where the ethic was the same: Let's see how much we can violate the law without getting caught. After all, winning is the only thing.

Right now, handball is very close to being totally a sport of honesty and sportsmanship, played to determine the most skilled practitioner, not the cleverest at hoodwinking the referee and the rule book. I detect some tendencies to get away from this honorable state and to move toward the traditional sports war. With a little awareness now, those trends can be aborted and the game preserved as a true sport.

Games played on the playgrounds among friends change their character once referees are introduced and given power over the game. When two kids or adults play handball in a gym, or on the playground, it is extremely rare that they have disputes over calls. Using the method of mutual agreement, over 99 percent of the game is played without a problem. Where there is a disagreement over a point, it is usually resolved simply by playing it over.

When a referee is introduced, we make an unfortunate error. We allow him not only to resolve the 1 percent of calls in dispute, but also the 99 percent for which there is no problem. Invariably, some of these 99 percent generate problems. Many times both players know a call is wrong, but, because of the referee structure, resentments build up, injustices are felt, and many players are motivated to plan ways to take advantage of the referee's fallibility. They begin to succeed, and the inevitable complaint is for more competent referees.

The solution is simple. Stop this trend toward encouraging cheating by changing the rules to make mutual agreement among players override the verdict of the referee. The game would proceed as now with the referee making all the decisions. If both players disagree with the referee, the players prevail. If the referee feels that they misunderstood a rule, he could point that out to them, but the opinion of the participants still prevails. If the players disagree with each other, the referee's decision holds.

To my suggestion, objection is often raised that the method of mutual agreement gives an advantage to the unscrupulous players who would take advantage of an honest player's truthfulness and not reciprocate. This certainly raises a moral dilemma, the choice of being a dishonest champion or an honest loser. My feeling is that mutual agreement makes public the ethics of the players. It would become very evident to the players, who apparently already know, and to the spectators, who the honest and dishonest players are. The pressure would be very strong to play fairly.

Again, the suggested solution is simple, based on honesty, self-responsibility and awareness, and the principle of agreement.

My letter was received with mild interest.

## FELDENKRAIS

The Feldenkrais approach to the body[7] could revolutionize athletics. Moshe Feldenkrais believes that if I strain, my body is not being used properly. My body will do everything it is capable of doing. I must learn how to communicate with it.

When I perform strenuously, I must fight myself to achieve that performance. If Feldenkrais were taken seriously, almost everything in athletics would change, including the way I warm up, the way I exercise, the way I train, the achievement of flexibility, ideas about one-handedness, methods of learning complex movements, and the avoidance of injury.

Feldenkrais claims that I use my body at such a low level of efficiency that virtually every movement I make is done by a small number of muscles with the other muscles either not participating or actually opposing the movement. Strongly one-handed people exemplify this. A movement with the right arm, such as a tennis stroke, is usually inhibited by some of the muscles on the left side of the body. Feldenkrais's exercises are aimed at integrating all the muscles of the body so that movement is made most gracefully and with the least effort.

Graceful movement is accomplished through the nervous system, where impulses are sent to the muscles with a certain rapidity and in a certain sequence. Feldenkrais is saying that if I become aware of my body, I function with far greater efficiency and with far less effort. This is true not only for movement, but also for the other functions mediated by the nervous system: thinking, sensing, and feeling.

Reinforcement for Feldenkrais's ideas has come from an unexpected source. Children born "without violence" through the method of Frederick Leboyer[36] have been found, in eight-year follow-up studies, to be almost exclusively ambidextrous.

With Leboyer's method, children are born into a quiet atmosphere without bright lights. They are born naturally, no drugs having been given to the mother except in emergency. The infants are never hit or treated as though they have no awareness. They are given to the mother immediately, stroked and massaged, and bathed in body temperature water where they can relax, after their work, in an ambience that feels like what they have been used to since conception. They are gently introduced to silence and to stillness which, since they have resided for the gestation period in a living, gurgling, breathing, talking body, they have never known before. The purpose of all this is to give the infant a feeling of safety and lovedness, to make the infant feel fine and welcome, and to reduce the infant's anxiety.

This surprising finding of ambidexterity suggests that two-handedness may be the natural state for humans not traumatized at birth. One-handedness may be a safety response to the anxiety of infancy, a clinging to the first successful response. If there is no anxiety, both sides of the body may be explored and developed, leading to a more integrated organism.

Feldenkrais's view is that warm-up for physical activities is done best by never straining muscles, but rather moving them, repeatedly, up to their limit. Muscles release when standard patterns are broken and movements occur which utilize the independence of each muscle. This method is far more effective than those requiring strain, such as push-ups, jumping jacks, and other warming-up techniques.

Feldenkrais emphasizes body awareness. The key to avoiding injury and illness is awareness. Drawing on this fact, the approach to injury in athletic events would be reassessed. No longer would injured players be looked upon as suffering unfortunate accidents. The accidents are choices the players are making. Training in increased bodymind awareness would be used to minimize injury.

# EDUCATION

To follow the principles of profound simplicity, an educational institution would concentrate in two areas: (1) creating conditions most conducive to learning; and (2) allowing students maximum responsibility for their own learning. These principles reinforce some trends already evident in some educational institutions and suggest some new directions.

When I was in Israel, I saw the place where Jesus was born. I floated in the Dead Sea and visited Galilee and Bethlehem and Nazareth. I was fascinated. I had a strong desire to study the Bible. In all my years of education, I had never entertained anything resembling such a thought. The obvious was upon me. If I wanted to study the Bible, I should certainly be in Jerusalem.

The modern educational institution would abandon the idea of a large physical plant in favor of settings appropriate to the subject matter. The entire countryside is the classroom. Learn French in Paris or Montreal, astronomy at an observatory, botany in the fields, law in the courts. Do T'ai Chi and dance at the seashore; learn business in the financial district. It is not difficult nor unduly expensive to set up classroom environments in those locations rather than in a third-floor room in a university building.

Time segments are also flexible. A five-day residential workshop has the same number of hours as most one-semester courses. In encounter workshops, many of us have learned that in most cases massed meetings are far more effective than spaced ones. Conducting a group in an isolated setting, living together for one or two weeks, usually leads to far better learning than the same number of hours spread over months or years at one to three hours a week. The workshop format has the advantage of concentrating energy on one topic rather than disbursing it to many.

Varying site and tempo of classes is a simple change from normal school procedures. It can make an enormous difference in student motivation and understanding, and it may be accomplished with a minimum of alteration from a normal school offering and can, with a small amount of ingenuity, be done practically.

Enhancing student choice begins with awareness. Education has developed an unfortunate veneration of the remote. If, as a student, I want to learn of beef production in Argentina, or the history of the Essenes, or the cloud cover on Mars, I receive great encouragement and support from the educational establishment. However, if I want to know more about why I am reluctant to ask a question, or how I feel about my teacher, or what to do about my sexual feelings toward a classmate, I am in trouble. Here and now feelings are not a proper study for the traditional classroom.

The paradox is that these personal issues are the issues which preoccupy me and which are directly related to my choice to learn. If I feel stupid, I will be reluctant to ask any questions for fear of being publicly humiliated and exposed. If I dislike or fear my teacher, I might rebel against anything I am taught as an expression of resisting the teacher.

Failure to explore my present state also leads me to study subjects in which I have no interest. These considerations suggest a core experience in which I have an opportunity to explore myself and my own feelings in relation to what I am learning. I must increase my awareness of myself to be in touch with what I am ready to learn. I can then choose for myself what I wish to explore.

Awareness requires honesty. Student explorations would aim at discovering what is going on, not at evaluating students. Evaluation may be done by the students themselves. In all the courses I have taught recently, I have had the students give themselves grades at the end of the course and tell the class what they are giving themselves and why. Their grades are probably more accurate than my own, and they are not all A's. When I surrender the grading power, it usually makes it easier for the student to concentrate on learning rather than on performance.

Through personal awareness, I, the student, am in a position to create my own education. I can sense what I want to learn and how I want to learn it. The educational institution provides me with a variety of learning environments both in time and space. I now plan my own path. The role of the university or of the instructors is to be responsible for themselves, not for me. Rather than tell me what subjects I can take, they simply decide whether they will cooperate with my proposal, if they will give me a degree, whether they require more, or whatever. In this way, I negotiate my own learning.

The modern educational institution thus creates conditions optimal for students to learn and provides many options. The students become aware, learn honesty through acquaintance with their total beings, and take responsibility for their own growth.

# FAMILY

## MARRIAGE

Bhagwan Shree Rajneesh, the Indian guru from Poona, was reported to have said that one must learn to love another before one could love oneself. This is the opposite of all I have believed since first reading Erich Fromm. Yet when I heard Bhagwan's statement, I immediately knew that he was right. I had no logical justification. It just felt correct.

When I lived alone, I could come to terms with myself fairly well. However, when I entered into a love relationship, many aspects of myself were revealed that never surfaced when I was alone. I never felt so much anger or desire for revenge. I never felt so much love and fulfillment. I was never forced to examine feelings that I was amazed to see as part of me. In short, the relation elicited aspects of my personality that I was not aware of when I lived alone.

The profound simplicity relation between members of a couple is, at minimum, honest. Honest marriage, rather than monogamy or open marriage, is the ideal. Each person takes responsibility for the self, and joint behavior is done by explicit agreement. An open marriage is possible if that is what both people, with awareness, desire. They may also choose to be monogamous, to have a double standard, or to make any arrangement on which they both agree.

Society's role, again, is to create and simplify the selection of options. Legal marriage is one option. Other living arrangements are made simpler by bestowing the approval of society on any of them. Divorce is also an option by mutual agreement. The concept of no-fault divorce, now being more widely accepted, is consistent with the present approach. The necessity for two people to prove the value of a divorce to a third person is absurd, wasteful of public funds, and wasteful of the time and energy of judges.

## CHILDREARING

Honesty and choice are the keynotes of childrearing also. Always telling the child the truth establishes credibility and assumes that the child is capable of coping with the world. My children were told that there was no individual named Santa Claus, but that it was fun to pretend that there was. I noticed no diminution of pleasure around Christmastime, I was spared the necessity of explaining the existence of multiple Santa Clauses, and my children and I were spared the disillusionment and discomfort of one day discovering that I had lied to them.

Being honest with children eliminates hundreds of decisions of "What shall we tell the children?" Many parents feel that children should be protected from knowledge of illness, divorce, bankruptcy, infidelity, or other foul deeds. In addition to helping the child remain dependent, this behavior is usually futile. Most children have at least a vague sense of something wrong and usually expend great amounts of energy trying to make sense of weird happenings.

Lack of honesty also may retard a child's awareness. The child will not be exposed to the world as it is and must overcome the lies in order to see the truth. Telling the truth to children also simplifies the parental relation. Intricate networks of lies and their corresponding tie-ups of energy are avoided.

Thus, following these principles, family relations are honest, each person being assumed to be responsible for himself or herself, everyone cooperating to stay aware and to reach explicit agreements on their mutual behavior.

## BIRTHING

Parenting begins before conception. Conception is the point at which life begins. The circumstances surrounding conception undoubtedly have an important influence on the fetus and, ultimately, on the child. Ideally, parents should start planning for the child before conception.

For my latest child, Ari, conception must have been a unique experience. His mother had fasted on water only, for 22 days. I had fasted for 34 days. The first time we made love after the fasts, Ari was conceived. Although my objectivity could be faulted, it seems to me that Ari is a particularly clear and radiant child.

I would certainly recommend something similar to all prospective parents. Fast, or otherwise purify your physical body—exercise, get plenty of sunshine and fresh air, be well rested, be physically fit, and deal with the emotional problems, both individually and interpersonally, between parents. In short, be in first-class condition in every respect just prior to conception. This may be the most important gift you give to your child.

Childbirth should be simple and self-responsible. That means using the natural childbirth methods developed so brilliantly by Grantly Dick-Read, Lemaze, and Leboyer.[36] As much as possible, childbirth should be directed by the mother. It should be without drugs and with a minimum of assistance. The child should emerge with equanimity and make an easy transition from the intra-uterine condition to the newborn state.

Drugs block the mother's energy cycle. Completion of the action of childbearing and of the feeling attendant on the moment of childbirth and after are stopped when the mother is not conscious at these times. The experience of birth is blocked for the infant, also, when the child is not fully awake during this crucial life experience. Regressed patients in groups frequently desire to re-experience their births because the drugs given to the mother stopped the completion of their energy cycles as well as those of their mothers.

Breast-feeding is a completion of pregnancy. The mother is provided by nature with the equipment necessary to develop the fetus to the point of birth and the infant to the point of weaning. The full energy cycle of birthing is conception to weaning. During this period, the mother creates the simplest and most nourishing conditions for the new life to enter the world. Any blockage of this cycle is felt in the infant and usually is the source of later problems or limitations for the child.

Modern child care often substitutes tragedy-avoidance for following the child's energy. Two-day-old Ari was subjected to a routine inspection by one of the most progressive doctors in outlandishly progressive northern California. And still it was a violation. With the greatest of gentleness, the doctor probed with stethoscope, took rectal temperature, squeezed testicles, stuck a Q-tip into eyes to take a culture to check on swollen eyelids. Ari was upset for two days.

Why were these probes necessary? They were not. The eyes were irritated because we foolishly allowed ointment to be put in the eyes "in case there is gonorrhea." The culture would be taken "in case there is conjunctivitis." The rectal temperature was taken "just in case there is infection." Shots will be given later "in case he should be exposed to various diseases." Bah!

All these procedures are based on the assumption that diseases are visited from without. Preventive medicine really means giving a small amount of the disease, or a buildup of resistance, to prevent serious disease. Virtually all preventive procedures are distressing, especially to infants like Ari. He is just getting used to the world and he is violated.

I assume that if Ari's life is agreeable, he will not

choose to be ill. If his parents are clear in their relation and within themselves, they will not create conditions Ari finds difficult to cope with. No unpleasant probes are needed, no drugs, no medicines, no traumas of any kind. Let him eat when he is hungry, be cleaned when dirtiness bothers him—not his parents—and have attention when he wants it. Let him explore his options. Let him become acquainted with his internal world so that he will not have to attend so many sensory-awareness groups when he is older. Let him pay attention to people when he wants to. Then, when he cries, it's a signal that he wants something, not a need for attention that he does not have satisfied in a direct way. If he is bothering you, let him know it. He can deal with reality.

Shots are rarely given for the infant; they are given for the protection of the parents and the doctor. They are one way of being "responsible," of avoiding criticism, or for avoiding lawsuits. What the infant seems to want is to be alone at times, to relate to someone at times, and to have his desires satisfied. I have never seen one who wants shots or probes.

Circumcision is another shocking practice of at least tragedy avoidance. It sometimes has a religious basis having to do with the regulation of sexual stimulation. Medical evidence, formerly thought to support the idea that cervical cancer in women is reduced if their men are circumcised, has been shown to be quite erroneous.[80] In regressing patients back to early years, Lowen[7] and others have concluded that circumcision is the origin of many emotional problems. It is another violation of the male infant.

The present approach would suggest this: Birth the child as naturally as possible. The Leboyer method is probably the most complete. Keep the relation between parents totally open and honest, and the awareness of each parent at the highest level. Follow the energy of the infant; do not regard him or her as the enemy, there to outwit the parents. Breast-feed and satisfy all the infant's needs as they arise, especially at the very beginning when the infant's conception of the world is being formed. Do not violate the child. No circumcision, shots, and the like except in the direst of circumstances. If you must have the child examined, have it done visually and pleasurably, avoiding even momentary displeasure.

This type of treatment is often called coddling and spoiling and is frowned upon because "the child should be prepared early for the rough life ahead." Nonsense! The more the child has all his or her desires met while young, the stronger will be the ego and the easier it will be for the child as an adult to cope with setbacks when they occur.

Recently, Liedloff[81] has made a major contribution to childrearing during the post-birth period. Borrowing from the Yequana Indians of South America, Liedloff recommends that children be held in arms 24 hours a day by someone, mainly, but not always, the mother, until the child no longer wants it, a period of usually six to eight months. The child should also be slept with, and be present at intercourse, in short, included.

Following what she calls the continuum concept, Liedloff feels that this is the proper place for a newborn, citing numerous animals and primitive tribes which follow this practice. In a sense, it properly completes the birth process. Children cry when they are put down, she says, not because they are spoiled, but because they do not belong down there in the first place. Gratification of the in-arms need until the child voluntarily crawls off the lap and begins to creep, mitigates the need for a life-long quest to return to this secure state.

The continuum concept is a splendid example of the completion principle. Allow the child to complete the birth energy cycle and the child will be able to proceed through life without the need for constant return to finish the unfinished.

I am not recommending all of the above procedures for all parents. Only if you feel comfortable with this philosophy will they be optimal. If you are worried about disease, get shots. If you would be anxious without circumcision, have it done. Reduction of your anxiety is a sufficient reason to have these things done. If you are not anxious in these ways, then, I feel, the recommended procedures are very valuable.

# LIVING

Concepts like choice and total honesty are very foreign to my upbringing. They sound weird. So does the whole thrust toward self-enlightenment. Mine was a mildly Jewish, barely middle-class, broken home where such lofty ideas were rarely mentioned. Practicalities of life dominated the interaction.

I still feel on occasion that old reaction to the profound simplicity ideas. From that historical standpoint, all that I have written here is nonsense. I can hear my relatives saying to me: "Yes, this is all fine, bubbie, but why don't you just go out and get a nice job and stop worrying about such things?"

As my belief in these ideas increases, I feel changes in my way of being. With more honesty, I feel clearer and freer. Accepting that I choose my life leads me to feel more flowing. A great deal of tension is gone, and I feel more able to deal with whatever happens. Increased awareness leads to diminution of the grand mysteries. Life is not so complicated because now I see how I can influence it.

Growing into believing all of these principles makes me lighter. Life is less dark and morose. It is becoming more like a game in which I can step back at any time to watch how I am playing it. And I am beginning to learn how I can change the way I play it if I do not like what is happening.

With this background, I find that I keep reminding myself: It's good to be honest and aware, responsible and simple, and if I do not feel like being honest and aware, responsible and simple, it is all right. If you do not breast-feed, it is all right. If I go to a doctor, or eat ice cream, or get angry, frightened, and depressed, or do not exercise, it is all right. Knowing that these profound simplicity practices feel good does not mean that I must follow them all the time or any of the time. I do not have to feel guilty or evil. All that is happening is that I am not following them. That is all.

# ENDARKENMENT

Sometimes my striving toward growth becomes the object of amusement to the part of me that is watching me. A few years ago, I tired of enlightening myself.

For a while, at least, I just wanted to be closed and dishonest, to eat French-fried onion rings and get pimples, to eat a Sara Lee German chocolate cake and get fat. So I devised a workshop called Endarkenment to allow myself to do just that.

In Endarkenment, all the usual rules are changed. We spent a week being devious. Superficiality was in. So was trying to make a good impression, telling lies to get what we wanted, and blaming others for our problems. We asked questions instead of making statements, and said: "people think" instead of "I feel"; and "it" instead of "I"; "can't" instead of "won't"; and "I don't know" when we did not want to think about it. Hard drinking was encouraged, especially straight Scotch.

In the workshop, we taught people what to obsess about while meditating, and how to walk rigidly and breathe in a restricted manner. Smoking was encouraged, two cigarettes at a time. Grades were posted frequently. We had a blame session where group members thought of things they did not like about themselves. Then they blamed other group members for their troubles. "If you wouldn't crowd me so much, I could think better." Then they explained how their difficulties were the fault of the men or of the women in the group, of the leader, of the workshop, of the environment, of the economic situation in the country, of the political climate, of their parents, spouses, or role expectations, of their obligations, of what Nixon did to the country, and, of course, ultimately, of how everything bad in their lives was the fault of Almighty God.

The embarrassing revelation from this exercise was the ease with which we could think quickly of very logical reasons for each blame. The lesson is the pointlessness of the blame after it is all over. All that is left is the pleasure one can derive from blaming.

One startling conclusion from the workshop was that the result was almost the same as that of regular workshops. Awareness was the key. As people became aware of how they tortured themselves and of how they made themselves miserable, they also became aware of how not to do those things. They had a marvelous time caricaturing themselves and thereby getting a perspective on what seemed a very heavy aspect of life. Along with awareness came the realization of the human comedy and, combined with an understanding of choice, the realization that all of it was changeable.

One of the features of the workshop was the teaching sessions. Each person told the group their worst trait and then taught the rest of us how to acquire it. Probably the best Endarkenment player was the young man who told the group that his problem was not finishing things. He had started dozens of projects but had never found the time to complete them. On Wednesday afternoon, he would teach the group how not to finish things. Wednesday afternoon came and he had dropped out of the workshop.

When life seems to be very, very heavy, and I seem to be taking myself very, very seriously, I look at myself and I think of the phrase of James Joyce: *"Nos ad manum ballum jocabimus."*

"Let's go play handball."

# EPILOGUE

"Sure wish Ari had remained articulate a minute longer. I wanted to ask him one more thing."

"You wish what?" said his mother.

"Well you see I had a little fantasy that Ari explained things to me. . . ."

"Um humm . . . What didn't he, uh, explain to you?"

"If we do become aware and honest and self-responsible and natural—what then? Isn't it a drag? Doesn't it weigh us down? Isn't life heavy and always probing? What happens to a person who finally reaches that point?"

"Too bad he can't answer, unless . . ."

"Unless what?"

"Unless you'll accept a nonverbal answer."

"What do you mean?"

"Ari always seems to be having fun."

# NOTES

Numbers in parentheses refer to pages on which Notes are referenced.

1. Schutz, W. *Elements of Encounter.* New York: Bantam, 1975. (Original publication, 1973.) (3)

2. ———. *Body Fantasy.* New York: Harper and Row, 1977. (Original publication, 1976.) (3)

3. Brown, B. *New Mind, New Body.* New York: Bantam, 1975. (4)

4. Simonton, O., Simonton, S. and Creighton, J. *Getting Well Again.* Los Angeles: Tarcher, 1978. (4, 127, 165)

5. Geller, U. *Uri Geller, My Story.* New York: Praeger, 1975. (4)

6. Smith, A. *Powers of Mind.* New York: Ballantine, 1976. (5)

7. For introductions to these approaches see:
   Schutz, W. *Elements of Encounter, ibid.*
   Perls, F. *Gestalt Therapy Verbatim.* New York: Bantam, 1971. (Original publication, 1969.)
   Schutz. W. *Body Fantasy, ibid* (for rolfing).
   Schutz, W. *Here Comes Everybody.* New York: Harper & Row, 1972 (for rolfing).
   Rolf, I. *Rolfing: The Integration of Human Structures,* Boulder, Colorado: Rolf Institute, 1977.
   Berne, E. *Games People Play.* New York: Grove Press, 1964 (for Transactional Analysis).
   Steiner, C. *Scripts People Live.* New York: Bantam, 1975 (also for Transactional Analysis).
   Lowen. A. *Bioenergetics.* New York: Penguin Books, 1976.
   Lilly, J. *The Center of the Cyclone.* New York: Bantam, 1973 (for Arica).
   Benson, H. and Klipper, M. *The Relaxation Response.* New York: Avon, 1976.

Huang, A. *Embrace Tiger, Return to Mountain.* New York: Bantam, 1977 (for T'ai Chi).

Yamada, Y. *Aikido.* Cedar Knolls, New Jersey: Wehman, 1974.

Barlow, W. *The Alexander Technique.* New York: Knopf, 1973.

Feldenkrais, M. *Awareness through Movement.* New York: Harper & Row, 1973. (11)

Spino, M. *Beyond Jogging.* Berkeley: Celestial Arts, 1976.

Shelton, H. *Fasting Can Save Your Life.* Chicago: Natural Hygiene Press, 1964.

Vishnudevananda, S. *The Complete Illustrated Book of Yoga,* Vol. I and II. New York: Pocket Books, 1960.

Hoffman, B. *Getting Divorced from Mother and Dad.* New York: E. P. Dutton, 1976.

Prestera, H. and Kurtz, R. *The Body Reveals.* New York: Bantam, 1977.

Dychtwald, K. *Bodymind.* New York: Jove/HBJ, 1978.

Hubbard, L. *Dianetics.* Los Angeles: American Saint Hill Organization, 1973.

Orr, L. and Ray, S. *Rebirthing is the New Age.* Millbrae, California: Celestial Arts, 1977.

Janov, A. *Primal Man: The New Consciousness.* New York: Crowell, 1976.

Dass, R. *Be Here Now.* New York: Crown, 1971.

Assagioli, R. *Psychosynthesis.* New York: Viking Press, 1971.

Katinka Matson has compiled brief descriptions of all of these methods and more in *The Psychology Today Omnibook of Personal Development.* New York: Morrow, 1977. (5, 164, 189, 199)

8. Schutz, W. *Joy.* New York: Ballantine, 1973 (original publication, 1967). (8, 11)

9. The idea of total body awareness is described in Michael Murphy's book, *Jacob Atabet.* Millbrae, California: Celestial Arts, 1977. (9)

10. From *The Gospel of Peace of Jesus Christ by the Disciple John.* Berkeley, California: Shambala, 1970, p. 130. (17)

11. A few examples of individuals and/or organizations exploring holism:
*Wholistic Health and Nutrition Institute.* Mill Valley, California.
*Humanistic Law Institute.* Paul Savoy, John F. Kennedy University, Orinda, California.
*Holistic Politics.* John Vasconcellos, California State Assembly, Sacramento, California.

*Holistic Dentistry.* Stephen L. Gold, D.D.S., M.P.H. University of California School of Dentistry, San Francisco, California.
*Holistic Business.* Robert Schwartz, Tarrytown House, Tarrytown, New York.
*Holistic Sports* (see Note 78).
*Holistic Childbirth.* Leni Schwartz, Mill Valley, California. Center for Holistic Studies, Antioch University West, San Francisco, California. Will Schutz, Director. (17)

12. Greenberg, D. "Cancer: Now the Bad News," *Journal of the International Academy of Preventive Medicine.* Vol. II, No. 2, Second Quarter, 1975, pp. 23–29. (18)

13. The technique of guided imagery is extremely effective for the deep probing into and working through of difficult emotional problems. The method was first described in Desoille, R., *The Directed Daydream,* and in Leuner, H., *Initiated Symbol Projection,* both published in New York in 1965 by Psychosynthesis Research Foundation. The method is a major tool used in the story of *Body Fantasy, ibid.* (18, 74, 104)

14. Schutz, W. *Here Comes Everybody, op. cit.* (19)

15. Kelley, C. *New Techniques of Vision Improvement.* Santa Monica, California: Inter-science Workshop (now Radix), 1971. (20)

16. Rolfing is a method of deep massage aimed at realigning the body to be more consistent with gravity. Realignment leads to a relaxation of muscle tensions, an increase of movement and increased energy. The method is described in more detail in two of my books, *Body Fantasy* and *Here Comes Everybody,* and in Ida Rolf's book *Rolfing.* (21)

17. Blake, W. *The Marriage of Heaven and Hell.* Coral Gables, Florida, University of Miami Press, 1973. (25)

18. Feldenkrais, M. *Body and Mature Behavior.* New York: International Universities Press, 1970. (25)

19. Green, E. and Green, A. *Regulating our Mind-Body Processes.* Topeka, Kansas: Research Department, Menninger Foundation, 1973. (25)

20. McWhirter, N. and R. *Guinness Book of World Records.* New York: Bantam, 1976. (25)

21. Geller, U. *op. cit.* (27)

22. Roberts, J. *The Nature of Personal Reality*. New York: Bantam, 1978. (29)

23. Bradford, L. *National Training Laboratories: Its History 1947–1970*. Private publication, 1974. (29)

24. Schutz, W. *An Approach to the Development of Human Potential*. A report of the Continuing Human Relations Lab at Bethel, Maine, August 15, 1963. The other three workshop leaders were Charles Seashore, Herbert Shepard, and Robert Tannenbaum. (29)

25. Roberts, J. *The Seth Material*. New York: Bantam, 1976. Roberts, J. *Seth Journal*. New York: Bantam, 1974. Roberts, J. *The Nature of Personal Reality*. New York: Bantam, 1978. (30)

26. Axiom 10 from the Arica training by Oscar Ichazo. Available through Arica Institute, 57th Street and 5th Avenue, New York City, 10019. (30)

27. From the est (Erhard Seminars Training) training, written by Werner Erhard. (30)

28. Greenwald, H. *Direct Decision Therapy*. New York: Knapp, 1973. (30)

29. Reich, W. *Listen, Little Man*. London: Penguin, 1975 (original publication, 1948). (30)

30. Perls, F., Hefferline. R., and Goodman. P. *Gestalt Therapy*. New York: Dell, 1951. (30)

31. This is a gestalt therapy technique (see Perls, *et al., op. cit.*) in which a person talks to an aspect of self, in this case her guilt, and just says what comes spontaneously. She carries on a dialogue between herself and her guilt, playing both roles. She will change positions for each role, take on different voices and different postures if they occur spontaneously as she plays out the scenario. The technique is valuable for quickly discovering various factors underlying otherwise incomprehensibe feelings. (36)

32. This is a point made by Werner Erhard in the est training. (54)

33. Steiner, C. *op cit*. (54)

34. Miller, S., Remen, N., Barbour, A., Nakles, M., Miller, S., and Garell, D. *Dimensions in Humanistic Medicine*. San Francisco: Institute for the Study of Humanistic Medicine, 1975. (59)

35. Hall, M. *Man, the Grand Symbol of the Mysteries.* Los Angeles: Philosophical Research Society, 1947 (original, 1932), pp. 87–89. This book presents a comprehensive discussion of the occult views of anatomy and of the relation between anatomical laws and the laws of the universe. (60)

36. Dick-Read, G. *Childbirth Without Fear.* New York: Harper and Row, 1970.
    Karmel, M. *Thank You, Dr. Lamaze: A Mother's Experience in Painless Childbirth.* New York: Doubleday, 1971 (original publication, 1959).
    Leboyer, F. *Birth Without Violence.* New York: Knopf, 1975. (63, 190, 197)

37. Shelton, H. *The Hygienic Care of Children.* Chicago: Natural Hygiene Press, 1970. (Original publication, 1931.) (64)

38. For a detailed description and discussion of encounter groups see my *Elements of Encounter, op. cit.* (69)

39. Russell, B. and Whitehead, A. *Principia Mathematica,* Vols. 1–3. Cambridge, England: The University Press, 1925. (70)

40. There was a later controversy as to whether they actually accomplished their goal. See Godel, K. *On Formally Undecidable Propositions of Principia Mathematica and Related Systems* (translated by B. Meltzer). New York: Basic Books, 1962 (original publication, 1931). (70)

41. Thomas, L. *The Lives of a Cell: Notes of a Biology Watcher.* New York: Bantam, 1975. (72)

42. Shelton, H. *Fasting Can Save Your Life, op. cit.* (72, 73)

43. Shelton, H. *Natural Hygiene, Man's Pristine Way of Life.* San Antonio: Dr. Shelton's Health School, 1968. (73)

44. Rajneesh, B. *The Way of the White Cloud.* Poona, India: Rajneesh Foundation, 1976. (75)

45. For a description of this visit, see "Joy Meets Love in Poona," a cassette tape available from Big Sur Recordings, Big Sur, California 93920 (Attention: Paul Herbert). (76)

46. Feldenkrais, M. *op. cit.* There are many tapes of his exercises that are very useful. These may be obtained from Big Sur Recordings, Big Sur, California, 93920 (Attention: Paul Herbert). (90)

47. See Simeons, A.T.W. *Man's Presumptuous Brain*. New
York: Dutton, 1961.
Alexander, F. *Psychosomatic Medicine: Its Principles and
Applications*. New York: Norton, 1965.
For a more recent, popular account, see Lewis, H. and M.
*Psychosomatics: How Your Emotions Can Damage Your
Health*. New York: Pinnacle Books, 1975. (97)

48. Similar schema have been developed by:
Mead, G. *The Philosophy of the Act*. Chicago: University
of Chicago Press, 1972. (Impulse, Perception, Manipula-
tion, Consummation—the Act applied to social situations.)
Reich, W. *The Function of the Orgasm*. New York: Pocket
Books, 1975 (Tension, Charge, Discharge, Relaxation).
The steps of the Scientific Method are frequently described
as: Problem, Hypothesis, Test, Result.
The body types that follow, Toneless, Blocked, and
Armored, are roughly parallel to Lowen's Oral, Masochistic,
and Rigid respectively. See Lowen, A. *The Language of the
Body*. New York: Collier, 1971 (original publication, 1958).
(99)

49. This technique is explained and illustrated at length in
*Body Fantasy, op. cit.* (107)

50. This principle is described in *Body Fantasy, op. cit.* page
10. (108)

51. The theory using Inclusion, Control, and Affection (also
called FIRO theory) has been presented in progressively
evolving form in most of my books. Its first presentation
was in *The Interpersonal Underworld* (FIRO). Palo Alto:
Science and Behavior Books, 1966 (original publication,
1958). A review of many studies converging on these
three dimensions is presented in Chapter 2.
The most complete presentation, supported by empirical
research and applied to school administration, appears
in my *Leaders of Schools*. La Jolla, California: University
Associates, 1977.
There are several scales available to measure various
aspects of behavior, including FIRO-B (interpersonal be-
havior), FIRO-F (interpersonal feelings), FIRO-BC
(FIRO-B for children), LIPHE (relation with parents),
MATE (compatibility of couples), COPE (defense or
coping mechanisms), and VAL-ED (educational values).
All of these, plus a manual, *FIRO AWARENESS
SCALES*, are available from Consulting Psychologists
Press, 577 College Avenue, Palo Alto, California 94306.
(111, 127)

52. See Spitz, R. "Hospitalism: An Inquiry into the Genesis of Psychiatric Conditions in Early Childhood." In Anna Freud (ed.), *Psychoanalytic Study of the Child*. New York: Interntional University Press, 1945. (112)

53. Elvin Semrad is a training psychoanalyst and one of my first teachers of group process. The concept of a goblet issue is one that he developed and described to a group of us during a training session in Boston in the mid-1950s. (121)

54. Johnson, A., Shapiro, L., and Alexander, F., "A Preliminary Report on a Psychosomatic Study of Rheumatoid Arthritis." *Psychosomatic Medicine* 9(1947): 295. (127)

55. "Prayers at Synagogue Stave Off Heart Attacks." *Jerusalem Post*, February 29, 1971. This is a report of the Israel Ischemic Heart Disease Project. (128)

56. *Science News* (113:378-382). (128)

57. *The Interpersonal Underworld* (*FIRO*). *op. cit.* (131)

58. Glueck, S. and Glueck, E. *Unraveling Juvenile Deliquency*. New York: Commonwealth Fund, 1950. (132)

59. Kennan, G. *Encounter Magazine*, London, Fall, 1976. (141)

60. Elves, A. "The Crisis of Confidence in Social Psychology," *American Psychologist*, October, 1975, pp. 967–76. (142)

61. Ostrow, R. "No Substantial Drop in Crime for 5-10 Years," *Los Angeles Times*, Nov. 24, 1974. (142)

62. Dubin, R. "Assaulting the Tower of Babel," review of Argyris, C., *Behind the Front Page*, in *Contemporary Psychology*, V. 20, No. 11, 1975. (142)

63. Carlson, R. *The End of Medicine*. New York: Wiley, 1975. (142)

64. Sommer, R. *The End of Imprisonment*. New York: Oxford, 1976. (142)

65. Gerald Ford, quoted in *Time Magazine*, August 23, 1976, page 21. (147)

66. Rhodes, J. *The Futile System. How to Unchain Congress and Make the System Work Again*. New York: Doubleday, 1976. (147)

67. Mill, J.S. *On Liberty*. New York: Norton, 1975 (original publication, 1912). (153)

68. Greacen, J. "Arbitration, A Tool for Criminal Cases? A Proposal for Bringing the Wisdom of Civil Settlements into Our Criminal Justice System." Available from National Institute of Law Enforcement and Criminal Justice, Washington, D.C. (154)

69. From, *Improving California's Mental Health System: Policy Findings and Recommendations* (p. 46). Calif. Assembly Permanent Subcommittee on Mental Health and Developmental Disabilities, Jan. 31, 1978. (155)

70. "Is It Time To Give Up On Prisons?" *San Francisco Chronicle*, May 4, 1976. (158)

71. "Former Felons Plan for Social Reform is Urged in New Norton Book." Interview with John Maher of Delancey Street. *Publishers Weekly*, 208: 54–55, December 29, 1975. (159)

72. Glasser, R. *The Body Is the Hero.* New York: Random House, 1976. (162, 164)

73. McQuade, W. and Aikman, A. *Stress.* New York: Bantam, 1975. (163)

74. Reich, W. *The Concept of Space* (V. Carfagus, translator). New York: Farrar, Straus and Giroux, 1958. (170)

75. Marin, P. "The New Narcissism." *Harper's Magazine.* December, 1975, pp. 45–50. (170)

76. *Ebony* magazine, August, 1978. (184)

77. New Games Foundation, Fluegelman, A. (ed.). *New Games Book.* New York: Doubleday, 1976. (185)

78. See Murphy, M. *The Psychic Side of Sports,* Reading, Pa.: Addison-Wesley, 1978. Similar approaches to sport are described in: Leonard, G. *The Ultimate Athlete.* New York: Avon, 1977; Gallwey, W. *The Inner Game of Tennis,* 1974; and Spino, M. *Beyond Jogging.* (186)

79. *Handball Magazine,* Sept., 1975, letter to the editor. (187)

80. Bryk, F. *Circumcision in Man and Woman: Its History, Psychology, and Ethology* (translated by Bergen, D.). New York: American Ethological Press, 1974 (original publication, 1934).
Lake, A. "Circumcision: Is It Necessary?" *McCall's Magazine,* 103:36, June, 1976. (199)

81. Liedloff, J. *The Continuum Concept.* London: Futura, 1975. (200)

# INDEX

Abdicrat, 117
Acupuncture, 149
Adler, 133
Affection, summary of expression of, 137
Affection behavior, 118–19
Aggression, 150–51
Aikido, 62–63
Aliveness, 86–89
Allopathic medicine, 165–66
Ambidexterity, 190
Amyotropic lateral sclerosis (Lou Gehrig's disease), 128
Anal development stage, 112
Arica, *quoted*, 31; 90
Art, 134
Astigmatism, and holism, 20
Astrology, 63
Autocrat, 117
Awareness, 98–93
　and body control, 93–94
　definition, 80
　and honesty, 193–94
　lack of, and illness, 94–95
　personal, 4
　revolution, 3–5
　rewarding, 150
　and student choices, 193

Bailey, Alice, 64
Bannister, Roger, 26
Bannister effect, 26
Basic dimensions, 111–37
　principles of, 111
Behavior, responsibility for, 43–44
Belief, 9–13
Benchley, Robert, 176–77
Berkeley Free Speech Movement, 170
Bioenergetics, 126
Biofeedback, 4, 94
Biorhythms, 63
Birthing, 197
Body, influence on choices, 40–41
Body awareness, 191
Body folk wisdom, 92
Body manipulation, 67–68
Bodymind, unfolding of, 98
Bodymind problems, 104–06
Body-mind unity, and cancer, 17–18
Body tissue, and personality, 20–21
Breast-feeding, 198

Cancer, 126–27
　self-healing, 165
Carson, Johnny, 88
Cheating, 35
Child discipline, 65
Childbirth, methods, 63–64
Childhood, 131–32
Childrearing
　and honesty, 196–97
　keynotes of, 196
Children, 64–66
Chinese philosophy, non-individual-istic, 77
Choice, 29–59
　awareness of, 34–35
　and caring, 46
　concept of, 30–32
　of death, 53–55
　of illness, 53–55
　incompleteness of, 60–61
　and parents, 37–38
　of rape, 49–53
　and spontaneity, 57–58
　of truth, 83
　yin of, 60–62
　yin and yang of, 78
Choice principle, 41
　and relationships, 58
Choices
　nonevaluative, 40
　and self-concept, 40
Circumcision, 199
Commitment, and group relations, 114
Community, 76–78
　as source of joy, 78
　conflict in, 76
Compassion, 42–44
　definition, 42
　factors determining, 42
　and responsibility, 42–43
Competence, 117
Competition, 185–86
　deleterious, 185
　transcended, 185–86
Continuum concept, 200
Control, summary of expression of, 137
Control behavior, 116–17
　manifestation of, 116
　problems in, 116–17
Crime, 152–54

215

Culpability, 55–57
  and law, 55–56

Death, 53–55
  with dignity, 167
  as suicide, 53–54
Decision making, 71–72
  and outside intervention, 58
Decision making process, 116
Delancey Street organization, 159
Delinquency, 132
Democrat, 117
Democratic tradition, 147–48
Dewey, John, 8
Dick-Read, Grantly, 63–64
Doctor, role of, 165–67
Dorsett, Tony, *quoted,* 184
Drugs, and childbirth, 197–98
Dualism, retreat from, 17

Education, 192–94
  and evaluation, 193–94
  and traditional classroom, 193
Emerson, Ralph Waldo, *quoted,*
    111
Emotional illness, of nations, 106
Emotional problems, types of, 104
Empathy, 45–47
Encounter, 73, 169–70
Encounter therapy, 33, 35
Encounter workshops, 192–93
Endarkenment, 43, 204–05
*End of Imprisonment, The,* 142
*End of Medicine, The,* 142
Energy cycle(s), 98–104
  abortion, 105
  action, 101–02
    denial of, 101
    distortion of, 101–02
  blockage in, 99
  completion of, 106–10
  and drugs, 196–97
  end result of, 99
  feeling, 102–04
    denial of, 102–03
    distortion of, 103
  motivation, 99–100
    denial of, 99
    distortion of, 99–100
  preparation, 100–01
    denial of, 100
    distortion of, 100
Energy flow, 66–68
Erhard, Werner, 30, *quoted,* 31
Evaluation, and choice, 35–37

Family, 195–201
  normal, 8–9
Fantasy, guided, 165
Fasting, 73–74, 91
*Fasting Can Save Your Life,* 73
Fears, prior experience of, 92
Feeding, solid food, 64
Feldenkrais, Moshe, 67
Feldenkrais technique, 11, 72–73,
    89–92, 189–91
*Final Days,* 84
FIRO-B, 127
Fisk, Carlton, 186
Ford, Betty, 87
Freud, Sigmund, 133
Freudian revolution, 70–71

Fromm, Erich, 195
Full disclosure law, 156

Geller, Uri, 26–27
Genital development stage, 112
Gerald Ford syndrome, 80
Gestalt therapy, 54
G.I. Bill, 178–79
Glasser, R., *quoted,* 162
Goblet issues, 121
Gossip, public reaction to, 85
Grange, Red, 62
Grantly Dick-Read method, 197
Greenwald, Harold, *quoted,* 31
Griffin, Merv, 61
Group development
  affection phase, 122
  control phase, 121–22
  cycling, 122–23
  inclusion phase, 120–21
  separation, 124–25
Group formation, basic dimensions
    of, 113
Group process, 69–70
  and interpersonal needs, 70
  principles of, 71
Guided fantasy, for cancer, 165
Guilt, and another's death, 55
*Guinness Book of World Records,*
    25
Guru-oriented techniques, 89–91
Gurus, roll of, 90

Hall, Manly Palmer, *quoted,* 60
Healing, and body's cooperation, 59
Health, 93–97
  aids to, 63
Hearst, Patty, 56–57
Helping, 44–45
Henley, William Ernest, 34
Hepatitis, meaning of, 95–96
Heroes, private lives of, 84–85
Holism, 17–24
  and eyesight, 18–20
  and illness, 17–18
Holistic approach, fundamental di-
    mensions of, 11
Holistic medicine, treatment phi-
    losophy in, 59
Homeopathic principle, 108–09
Honesty, 81–83
  definition, 80
  disadvantages of, 82–83
  and feelings, 82–83
  and sociological ills, 86
Human behavior, as series of ener-
    gy cycles, 98–104
Human potential, 25
  realization of, 4–5
Human potential movement, 171
Human potential techniques, 72–73
  applications of, 5, 6
  principles underlying, 6
Humphrey, Hubert, 127
Hyperthyroidism, meaning of, 97
Hypocrisy, 83–85

Ichazo, Oscar, 90
Illness, 93–97
  affection, 128–30
  cause of, 97
  choice of, 53–55

choice of specific, 125–29
  control, 127–28
  genital, 120
  inclusion, 125–27
  and lack of awareness, 94–95
  as learning experience, 168
  meaning of, and hepatitis, 95–96
  personal responsibility for, 163–166
  psychosomatic, 95–97
Imagery, 74–75, 91
  guided, 74–75
  mental, 73
Imagery methods, 19
I-nature, 133–34
Inclusion, summary of expression of, 137
Inclusion behavior, 114–16
Inclusion period, 112
Independence, and welfare, 178
Individual behavior, principles of, 71
Individual development, 112
Insecurity, and lying, 84
Interpersonal needs, 70
I-thou, 135–36

Joy, 88
Joy
  defined, 11–12
  full experience of, 19
  as life goal, 8–9
Jung, 133

Karen Quinlan case, 167
Karma, 38
Kennan, George, quoted, 141
Kennedy, John, 84, 106

Lamaze, 63–64
Lamaze method, 197
Law, 149–61
  unity of, 71–72
Leboyer, Frederick, 190
Leboyer method, 63–64, 190, 197, 199
Leukemia
  interpreted, 96
  national, 96
Liberation movements, 41
Licensing, 155–57
Liedloff, Jean, 200
Life-changing experiences, in illness, 168
Life goals, 8–9
Limitlessness, 25–28
Limits, imposed on children, 27
Living, 202–03
Loss, 37
Lou Gehrig's disease. See Amyotropic lateral sclerosis
Lying
  defined, 155
  effect on body energy, 79
  effect on life experiences, 86–89
  kinds of, 83
  reasons for, 84

McCarthy, Senator Joe, 127
Machiavelli syndrome, 79
Maconochie, Alexander, 158
Mantle, Mickey, 85

Mariage, as option, 195–96
MDA, 72
Medicine, 162–69
  physicion vs. patient, 163–64
Mental imagery, 73
Mill, John Stuart, quoted, 153
Merton, Thomas, 158
Myopia, and holism, 19

Narcissism, 171–75
National Enquirer, 85
National Training Laboratories (NTL), 29
Natural energy and fasting, 73
Natural Hygiene group, 73
Naturalness, 72–73
New Games philosophy, 185

Olympic Games, 160
Options, 38–39, 89–90
  conditions favoring, 39
  consequences of, 92–93
  reduction of, 62
Overpersonal behavior, 119
Oversocial behavior, 115

Parent-child interaction, 132
Parenting, beginning of, 197
Parents, 37–38
  choice of, 28
  conditioning of, 38
Perls, Fritz, quoted, 30, 31, 54
Personal behavior, 119
Personal significance, 114
Personality
  body tissue, and holism, 20–21
  levels of, 21
Politics, 170–83
Principia Mathematica, 70
Principle of Basic Dimensions, 111
Principle of completion, 98–110
Principles of application
  agreement, 144
  awareness, 146
  choice, 145
  freedom, 144
  goal, 144
  options, 146
  self-responsibility, 146
  simplicity, 145
  transition, 146–48
  truth, 145
Prison reform, 158–61
Privacy, 83–85
Psychoanalysts, 133
Psychological defenses, and body tensions, 21

Quality of life, methods for improving, 5

Rajneesh, Bhagwan Shree, 75–76, 195
Rape, and choice principle, 49–53
Re-experiencing technique, 109
Referees, 187–89
Reich, Wilhelm, quoted, 31, 170
Religion, 134
Revolution(s)
  awareness, 3–5
  movement of humanity toward, 3–6

Revolution(s) (con't.)
    new, 3, 6
    scientific, 4
    social, 3
Revolutionaries, paranoid behavior
    of, 106
Rorschach projective test, 93
Rose, Pete, 186
Roseto town, illness and communi-
    ty, 128–29
Rossman, Mike, 170
Russell, Bertrand, 70

Schizophrenigenic situation, 23–24
Science, 134
Self-awareness
    and health, 63
    techniques for increasing, 89–92
Self-compassion, 47–49
Self-concept, 40
Self-fulfilling prophecies, 29–30
Self-healing, by bodymind, 164
Self-oriented techniques, 89–92
Self-responsibility, 30, 44
    principle of, 131
    and rehabilitation, 158
Sex, 130–31
    affection aspect of, 131
    control aspect of, 130–31
    inclusion problems in, 130
Shakespeare, William, quoted, 31
Shelton, Herbert, 64, 73
Simplicity, 63, 60–78
    and understanding, 68–70
Smith, Adam, 5
Social behavior, 115–16
Social imbalances, basic dimensions
    of, 111
Social institutions, 135, 141–43
Social minorities, 41
Socialization era, 112
Society, 39–41
    and choices, 40–41
Spontaneity, 57–58
    and dishonesty, 82
Sports, 184–91
    competition, 185–86

Feldenkrais approach, 189–91
    referees, 187–89
Suicide
    and choice of death, 53–55
    responsibility for, 168–69
Suppression, 109
Swedenborg, Emanuel, quoted, 98

Tax board, functions, 180–82
Taxation, 179–83
    purpose, 180
    and self-responsibility, 182
Teaching, 75–76
Television, as giant society, 159–60
Tempest, The (Shakespeare), 31
T-groups, 29
Thurstone, L. L., 93
Transactional analysis (TA), 54
Transcendant experience, 186
Truth, 79–97
    definition, 80
    freeing effect of, 79–80
    and interpersonal richness, 82
    and spontaneity, 82
    and violence, 86
Tyranny of groups, 32–33

Unawareness
    and choice, 34–35
    rewarding, 149
Underpersonal behavior, 118–19
Undersocial behavior, 114–15
Understanding, three phrases of,
    68–70
Universe, simplicity of, 68

War, 86
Warren Commission, 106
Watergate, 106
Welfare, 176–79
Whitehead, Alfred North, 70
Wolf, Stewart, 128

Yang, of choice, 78
Yin, of choice, 78
Yoga, Western, 184